WORLD OF DOUGHNUTS

WORLD OF DOUGHNUTS

MORE THAN 50 DELICIOUS RECIPES FROM AROUND THE GLOBE

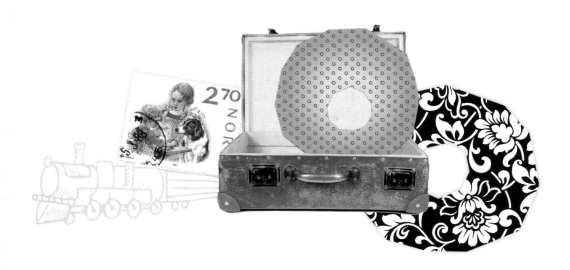

BY STEPHANIE ROSENBAUM

Photographs by Jenifer Altman

EGG&DART®

For my mother Leslie,
my father Jack,
and my sisters Michele
and Amy: Here's to
all those mornings at
the Downyflake.

ACKNOWLEDGMENTS

MANY THANKS to my longtime friend and extremely talented colleague Leslie Jonath, who made this project happen, and whose cheerful encouragement and great ideas have kept me cooking and writing throughout the years. I am very grateful to publisher Pam Senk Falk for turning her doughnut obsession into a passion for this project; to managing editor Lisa McGuinness for keeping the manuscript on track with such good humor; and to copyeditor Carolyn Miller for her line-by-line attention and care. Much of the charm of this book is due to the wonderful work of both designer Tracy Sunrize Johnson and photographer Jenifer Altman. I am thankful to all the friends who were willing to taste-test these doughnuts with me, especially Molly, Randy, Jackie, Shar, Ches, Kai, and Jen. Finally, the inspiration and support I've received over the years from the Writers' Colony at Dairy Hollow in Eureka Springs, Arkansas—and the time I've spent cooking, writing, and teaching in their beautiful Culinary Suite—has been a great boon to my creative life.

CONTENTS

INTRODUCTION

WHO DOESN'T LOVE A DOUGHNUT?

Cupcakes may be cute, cookies sweet, but doughnuts, glazed or raised, frosted or sprinkled, are *fun*. Sometimes, they're even downright goofy: just look at the names of some of our favorite doughnut shops. Sure, there are still plenty of Formica-counter joints named after Bob, Ann, or Betty Ann, but now these down-home spots are getting some sassy competition. In Portland, Oregon, clubbers hit Voodoo Doughnut for a late-night sugar rush, while Mainers line up for the Cheddar-bacon, sweet-potato ginger, and dark chocolate–sea salt doughnuts at the Holy Donut in Portland. In San Francisco, guys in goatees ride their bikes through the Mission District for the maple-bacon treats sold through the window at Dynamo Donuts. Or they cross the bridge to the East Bay to go old-school at Elmwood's Dream Fluff Donuts, or snack on the new and stylish sweets dished out at Oakland's Donut Savant and Doughnut Dolly.

In Seattle, vegans swear by the glazed and sprinkled rounds at Mighty-O. In San Jose, Psycho Donuts bills itself as "crazy good." In the Twin Cities of Minneapolis and St. Paul, Mojo Monkey Donuts boasts that its mango-glazed organic coconut doughnuts are something that "only a monkey can deliver," while others get their sugar on at Mel-O-Glaze Bakery or Minnetonka's YoYo Donuts. Utah's Beyond Glaze swears that its maple-bacon and bacon-chocolate doughnuts are "so delicious, you'll hate the hole." In Clare, Michigan, the historic Clare City Bakery morphed into the catchier Cops & Doughnuts when that century-old business was bought, and renamed, by nine local policemen.

Doughnut trucks hawk their wares from street corners, while classic doughnut shops still advertise themselves with doughnut-round signs the size of truck tires. Search along old highways and you might even find a few vintage-1950s doughnut shops built in the shape of giant doughnuts.

Add in the names of the doughnuts themselves—like Grape Ape (dunked in powdered grape drink mix), Nutella the Hun, Feather Boa, Cocoloco—and you know that while doughnut lovers take loyalty to their favorite doughnuts and doughnut shops pretty seriously, doughnuts themselves are a giggle, a hoot, a sweet treat for the kid in all of us.

And while doughnuts studded with breakfast cereal or topped with maple-glazed bacon may be uniquely American inventions, doughnuts of all shapes and sizes are eaten around the world. If there's a culture that *doesn't* fry up dough and roll it in something sweet or savory, well, we haven't found it yet. From Mexico up through California, street vendors hawk the long, thick or thin cinnamon twists known as churros; in Spain, the same pastries get dipped in pudding-rich hot chocolate as the perfect so-late-it's-early pick-me-up. Beignets may have gotten their start in Paris, but it's New Orleans that really made them famous, washed down with café au lait as this sultry city's best-loved breakfast treat. From China to Chinatown, Cantonese-style breakfasts start with hot bowls of savory rice porridge, known as congee or jook, served with unsweetened, freshly fried strips of dough.

Throughout the Near East, from Greece and Turkey to Syria and Lebanon, fried twists and balls of dough are soaked in honey syrup, flavored with rose water, orange-flower water, or cinnamon. They might be dolloped with thick yogurt, scattered with chopped pistachios or almonds, served with sweet, inky black coffee or hot mint tea. In Central and South America, doughnuts feed a sweet tooth with fillings of guava jelly, sweet cheese, gooey dulce de leche, or rich custard.

You can follow colonization, relocation, and immigration histories on a waft of sugar and spattering fat, as Portuguese malasadas were re-created by third-generation settlers in Hawaii, as German fasnachts were sizzled into Pennsylvania Dutch funnel cakes, and Viennese jelly doughnuts became Israel's sufganiyots.

Whether fried over a propane burner in a Bangkok alleyway or set out under fluorescent lights in an all-night coffee shop in Cleveland, doughnuts have long had a reputation as the workingman's treat, a fast, cheap, and sweet coffee-break staple for cops, shift workers, secretaries, and truck drivers.

Lately, however, doughnuts have gotten a fine-dining makeover. In California, The French Laundry, routinely called one of the best restaurants in the world, has made Coffee and Doughnuts one of its signature desserts. Of course, chef/owner Thomas Keller's version has never seen the inside of a Dunkin' Donuts. Instead, his "coffee" is a velvety frozen cappuccino semifreddo, his doughnuts petite sugar-dusted rounds fried just moments before serving. The British molecular-gastronomy genius Heston Blumenthal adds smoked potato to his batter, then coats the finished doughnuts with a caramelly dulce de leche glaze flavored with potato skin and studded with Pop Rocks candy. In dozens of flavors from bananas Foster to Valrhona chocolate, fried-to-order beignets have become the signature item for high-end pastry chefs in many cities.

Doughnuts can be fancy. Doughnuts can be hip. In Los Angeles, early-morning film shoots are fueled with "fauxnuts," doughnut lookalikes that are baked rather than fried, created and named by healthy baker Mani Niall, made vegan or even gluten-free. You can savor an artisanal handmade doughnut at your favorite coffee shop one day, then dive into a dozen packed in a cellophane-windowed box from an all-night convenience store the next. Slathered in salted caramel, piped full of passion-fruit cream, used as the base for sundaes and bread puddings, glazed and filled with everything from Tahitian vanilla to Tang, doughnuts are resilient. They roll high, they roll low. They're never out of style.

They're also a lot of fun to make. Drop raw dough into hot oil, and in less than five minutes, you'll have a freshly fried treat better and fresher than anything you'll find in a bakery. Plus, it's amazing to watch every time. It sinks, it sizzles, it flips, it's done! You've just made a batch of hot homemade doughnuts for everyone in the house. No need to be a highly trained doughnut engineer with a degree from Krispy Kreme U—all it takes is a little attention, a heavy pot, and a deep-fry thermometer. Follow these reliable recipes to get the hang of home-frying, and then let your imagination run wild. There's a world of flavor out there, just waiting to be fried, glazed, iced, and sprinkled to your belly's content. Okay, so we wouldn't put pickles and baloney in a doughnut. But maple-bacon doughnuts? You bet!

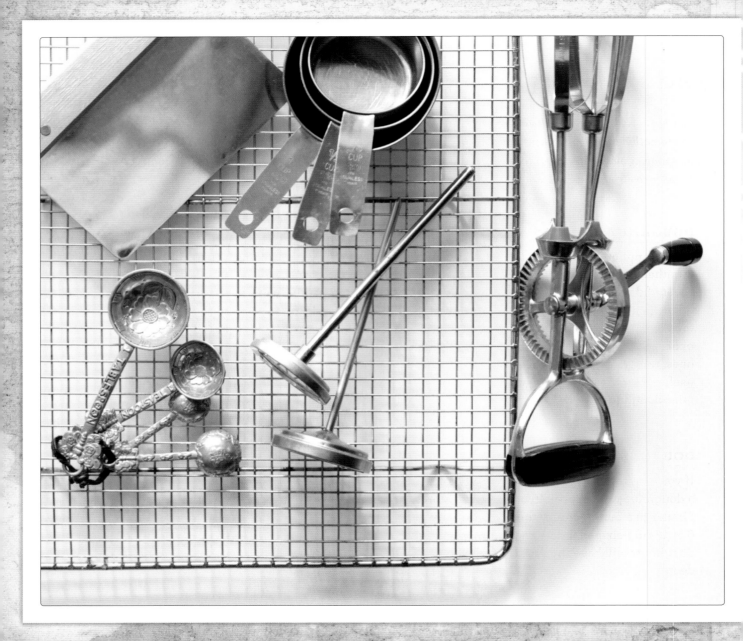

EQUIPMENT

You don't need to trick out your kitchen like a professional doughnut shop to make these recipes at home.
The three things you'll need? A wide, heavy pot (cast iron works best) for frying; an inexpensive metal doughnut cutter,
for stamping out uniform rings every time; and a slotted spoon or skimmer, to scoop your finished doughnuts from
hot oil to cooling rack with ease.

DOUGHNUT AND BISCUIT CUTTERS

A doughnut cutter is just two biscuit cutters put together, one small, one large. Stamp it into a sheet of dough, and you get a neat round with the hole already cut out. You can find these, usually for about $5 each, in most cookware stores. A set of biscuit cutters also comes in handy. The small ones, 1 to 1½ inches in diameter, are especially useful when you're making doughnut holes or mini-doughnuts.

DOUGHNUT PAN

If you'd rather bake your doughnuts, look for a doughnut pan in specialty housewares stores. Similar to a muffin pan, doughnut pans have 6 or 12 ring-shaped indentations, so your baked doughnuts will have the same shape as their deep-fried cousins.

ELECTRIC FRYER

Should you buy an electric fryer? The heating element regulates the temperature automatically, so you don't have to monitor heat levels before and during frying. It really depends on how much you plan to fry, and how much storage space you have in your kitchen. Our advice? Start by using a pot you already have, and move on to an automatic fryer only if you think you'll use it enough to justify the space it will take up in the cabinet. One exception: If you have an electric stove, you may find buying an electric deep fryer to be worth the price (and space). Because the coils on an electric stove are slower than gas flames to respond to changes in temperature, adjusting the heat under a pot of hot oil on an electric stove can be frustrating. An electric deep fryer can save you the trouble of moving a pot of hot oil on and off the coil trying to get the temperature right.

GRID RACK

Doughnuts need to drain off their excess oil when they come out of the fryer. The easiest way to do this is on a grid-patterned wire rack placed on a baking sheet. The crisscross grid supports the hot doughnuts more evenly than a typical wire rack with parallel wires.

ICING SPATULA

This long, flat, narrow metal spatula is great for spreading icing and glazes evenly over your doughnuts.

MICROPLANE

Adapted from a wood file, this inexpensive kitchen tool grates citrus, coconut, and hard spices quickly, easily, and without waste. You can find it in cookware stores in a variety of sizes and grating levels.

PASTRY BAG

For filling doughnuts with cream, custard, or jelly, the best tool is a pastry bag. Use a plain round tip attached to a reusable cloth or disposable plastic pastry bag filled with your filling of choice. Poke a hole in the side of the doughnut with the tip of a chopstick or a small sharp knife, insert the tip of the pastry bag, and squeeze in filling as needed. (This works only with doughnuts that don't have holes.)

POTS AND PANS

Small-batch doughnut frying doesn't take a lot of specialized equipment. The most important item is a deep, heavy pot. This pot should be at least 4 to 5 inches deep. You'll be filling the pot with at least 2 to 3 inches of oil, so having 2 to 3 additional inches of depth will help prevent hot oil from splashing out onto the stove top (and burners) when you're dropping in the doughnut batter. The pot should wide enough to hold 3 to 4 doughnuts at a time without crowding.

The cheapest, easiest to find, and most durable material for your doughnut frying? Cast iron. A cast-iron Dutch oven with a lid makes the perfect doughnut fryer, and you can probably find one at your local hardware store. Heavy cast iron conducts and holds heat evenly, which means you won't end up with uneven "hot spots" as you fry. It also makes maintaining an even temperature easier. Though not as deep as a Dutch oven, a large cast-iron skillet or a heavy sauté pan is a good substitute. Enameled cast iron, as in Le Creuset, is also a good choice. If you don't use cast iron, look for other heavy-gauge cookware, like All-Clad or Calphalon.

SLOTTED SPOON, SKIMMER

Using a long-handled slotted spoon to remove doughnuts from the fryer lets excess oil drain back into the pot. You can also use a wire-mesh skimmer, like the kind used in stir-frying.

STAND MIXER

These sturdy, powerful electric mixers aren't cheap, but quality brands (like KitchenAid) last for a long time, and make fast, hands-off work of whipping, mixing, beating, even kneading. While they are a useful addition to any kitchen, all of the recipes in this book can be made by hand using a whisk and/or a wooden spoon, or by using a hand-held electric mixer.

THERMOMETER

An easy-to-read candy or fryer thermometer is a must when it comes to frying reliably. If your oil is too hot, your doughnuts can end up burned on the outside but raw in the middle. Too cool, and your doughnuts will sop up the oil and end up heavy and greasy. We've found that an instant-read digital probe thermometer is the easiest to read and takes the guesswork out of frying. Make sure your thermometer goes up to at least 400°F.

TONGS

Metal kitchen tongs are useful for dipping doughnuts and doughnut holes into glazes, and for avoiding smudgy fingerprints on glazed or decorated doughnuts when you're moving them from rack to serving platter. They're also handy for retrieving churros and funnel cakes from hot oil.

INGREDIENTS

As always, the better your ingredients, the better your doughnuts. Use real high-quality chocolate, fruit, spices, and nuts, and you'll be rewarded by big, bold flavors.

BAKING POWDER, BAKING SODA

These chemical leaveners react with moisture, heat, and acidity to release carbon dioxide into your batter, making the batter expand and giving lightness and loft to cake doughnuts. The key element of this basic science? Chemicals don't last forever! Before you start, look at the expiration date on the baking powder and baking soda on your shelf. Unless you bake very regularly, that little can or box has probably been sitting in your pantry through several Olympic Games, winter *and* summer. Using old, no-longer-active baking powder or baking soda is the quickest way to wreck your baking, so dump it down the sink (where it will help get rid of odors), and replace it with fresh stuff. To avoid a metallic or "tinny" aftertaste, look for aluminum-free brands of baking powder, such as Rumford or Bob's Red Mill.

CHOCOLATE

High-quality chocolate has a rich, complex flavor that can be fruity, smoky, or nutty. Some of the brands we like include Scharffenberger, Guittard, Ghirardelli, Valrhona, and Lindt. Unsweetened chocolate, also called baking chocolate, is just that: pure bitter chocolate, with no sugar added. Bittersweet and semisweet chocolates have additional sugar added, more for semisweet, less for bittersweet. Many brands of chocolate now list the percentage of cocoa mass on their labels; taste around and find the level (usually between 50 to 80 percent) that pleases you most.

COCOA

Pure, unsweetened cocoa powder should not be confused with hot-cocoa or hot-chocolate mix. Dutch-processed cocoa powder, such as Droste, has been treated with alkali to reduce its acidity, which makes it both darker and more full-flavored. However, a good-quality "natural" cocoa will also work well in any of these recipes.

FATS AND OILS

Canola, safflower, and sunflower oils are all clean, neutral oils that heat up to a high smoke point and fry well. Peanut oil also works well; just make sure that no one you're cooking for has a peanut allergy. You can also use a non-hydrogenated solid vegetable shortening, such as Spectrum Organics Shortening, made from palm oil, or a solid fat, such as lard. Frying oil or fat can be reused several times, as long as you strain out any solid bits in between to prevent the oil from absorbing a burned flavor from overcooked batter. After several uses, the oil will begin to darken and may make your doughnuts overly greasy. Let the oil cool, then pour it off into an empty can or bottle and replace with fresh oil. To avoid clogs, never pour grease down the sink, especially fats that are solid at room temperature.

FLOUR

These recipes were tested using unbleached all-purpose white flour. You can substitute whole-wheat pastry flour for part or all of the flour in cake doughnut recipes, but your final product will be a little heavier and denser than those made with white flour. While flours can vary in weight and volume, the most reliable way to measure flour by volume is the "dip and sweep" method. Scoop the appropriate dry measuring cup into your flour container and brush off the excess with the flat side of a table knife. Don't shake or pack the cup.

MILK, BUTTERMILK, SOUR CREAM, YOGURT

You'll get best results with these recipes using whole or 2 percent milk, preferably not ultra-pasteurized. Buttermilk, a cultured, low-fat milk product found in the dairy section of most supermarkets, has the taste and consistency of thin, drinkable yogurt. It adds moistness (without much added fat) and a slight, pleasant tang. If you can't find buttermilk, you can use a half-and-half mixture of plain yogurt and milk, beaten well. For best results, look for all-natural, full-fat plain yogurt made from milk and live cultures, without additional thickeners, pectin, or other additives. Sour cream, too, should be real, full-fat sour cream, made of cream and cultures, without thickeners or other chemical additives.

SPICES

Spices can vary dramatically in strength and flavor, depending on their source and freshness. For best results, buy small amounts of spices in bulk from a natural foods or ethnic grocery store, or look for a high-quality brand of jarred spices, such as Penzeys. The biggest favor you can do your spices? Don't store them over the stove! Prolonged exposure to heat and light will turn even the most expensive jar into a bottle of fancy dust, so keep your spices in a cool, dark place. Numerous recipes in this book call for freshly ground nutmeg. Nutmeg, once ground, loses its fragrant, peppery bite very quickly. By contrast, whole nutmegs—round brown balls about the size of a small marble—keep their flavor for a very long time. For best flavor, buy whole nutmegs and grate them to order, using a Microplane or the fine holes of a box grater.

SUGAR

Unless otherwise specified, the sugar used in these recipes is granulated white cane sugar. You may enjoy the slightly more mellow flavor of organic cane sugar, often labeled "raw" sugar, which is pale beige in color, with slightly larger crystals. Powdered sugar, also called confectioners' sugar, is used predominantly for icing, glazing, and dusting. It is not inter-changeable with granulated sugar. Because of its tendency to lump, powdered sugar should always be sifted before using.

YEAST

Use active dry yeast to make the yeast-raised doughnuts in this book. If you want a faster rise, you can substitute rapid-rise yeast. If you bake bread or make other yeasted baked goods frequently, it's more cost-effective to buy your active dry yeast in bulk (or in a jar) rather than in individual packets. For best storage, keep dry yeast in the refrigerator. For best results, check the expiration date on the yeast package or jar before you use it.

FRYING CAN BE FUN

Follow these tips, and you'll be frying without fear in no time.

1. BE PREPARED

First, tie back long hair, wear closed-toe shoes, and make sure you're not wearing anything loose or dangly (like a scarf, long necklace, or floppy sleeves) that could drop into the hot oil inadvertently. Organize your work space so that you have room around the stove or fryer to arrange trays and racks for raw and finished doughnuts. Make sure nothing easily flammable, like paper towels, is stashed too close to the stove.

ITEMS TO HAVE ON HAND:

- *A pair of thick oven mitts*

- *A box of baking soda
  (to help smother flare-ups)*

- *A kitchen fire extinguisher, if you have one*

- *A snug-fitting lid for your frying pot or pan*

- *A slotted spoon, a skimmer or tongs for dropping in/retrieving doughnuts from hot oil*

- *A floured baking sheet for holding raw doughnuts*

- *A baking sheet lined with a grid-patterned wire rack or paper towels for draining finished doughnuts*

- *Fillings, glazes, icings, and/or flavored sugars, as needed*

2. HEAT YOUR OIL

As mentioned on page 16, deep-frying is best done in a heavy pot or pan that's at least 4 to 5 inches deep. This depth will help keep oil from splashing out onto the stove when doughnuts are dropped in. When heating the oil, do not cover the pot or fryer.

How fast it will take your oil to heat up to frying temperature depends on two factors: the power of your stove and the heaviness of your pot. A typical home stove, on medium-high heat, can take from 10 to 15 minutes to heat oil to the temperature called for in most of these recipes, 350° to 375°F. However, if you have a high-powered restaurant-quality stove, like a Wolf or a Viking, you may find it only takes 5 to 8 minutes to heat your oil. It's important to know your stove. The first few times you fry, take the oil's temperature every couple of minutes, and make sure to take readings in several places around the pot.

Making heating adjustments on an electric stove can be a little more difficult, since the coils on electric stoves take longer to adjust to changes in temperature. In this case, you may find it easier to do your frying in an electric deep fryer.

3. STAY IN THE KITCHEN

Even once you have a sense of your stove's heating power, *never leave a pot of oil unattended on the stove*. If you have to leave the kitchen, turn off the stove *first*. Then cover the pot and push it to the back burner, away from curious little (or not-so-little) hands. Even off the heat, hot oil retains its temperature for quite a while, and splashes and spills can cause serious burns.

4. WATER AND OIL DON'T MIX

Make sure your pot is absolutely dry before you start heating your oil, and keep anything wet away from it. (Just rinsed sticky batter from your hands? Make sure to dry them well before you approach your pot of hot oil!) The moisture in your doughnuts will inevitably cause some hissing and splattering when the raw doughnuts first go into the oil. Always lower the doughnuts into the oil in a large spoon or skimmer, so that your hands won't get splashed or spattered with hot oil.

5. TOO HOT, TOO COLD, JUST RIGHT

Maintaining an even oil temperature through the cooking process is a key part of making perfect doughnuts. Let your oil get too hot, and the outside of your doughnuts will brown (or burn) too fast, leaving the inside raw and gooey. If your oil isn't hot enough, the doughnuts will soak up too much oil and get greasy and soggy. Each time you add a batch of raw doughnuts to the oil, the temperature will drop, so check the oil temperature between batches to make sure it's correct.

Doughnuts with holes fry much faster than solid doughnuts. For best results, especially with solid ones, break open a "test doughnut" from your first batch to check how they're frying, and adjust the heat of your oil as needed.

6. KEEP AN EYE ON YOUR OIL

You can probably fry a dozen doughnuts in the same batch of oil. Depending on how much the doughnuts crumble in the oil, however, you may need to strain out excess particles before you finish frying, to keep them from burning and giving the oil (and doughnuts) an off flavor. (Be sure to wipe out your pot or pan with paper towels afterward to remove any excess oily sludge from the bottom.) Once your oil has cooled, you can strain it through a sieve lined with a paper towel into a clean can or bottle. If it doesn't have any off or burnt odors, you can probably use it to fry a couple more batches of doughnuts. However, if it's very dark or smells burned, it should be discarded.

To discard oil, let it cool, then pour it into a can or bottle for disposal in the trash. But first find out if your neighborhood offers cooking-oil disposal; some communities recycle used cooking oils into biodiesel. Never pour cooking grease or oil down the sink.

7. DRESS UP YOUR DOUGHNUTS

Once your doughnuts are fried, they're ready to dress up. Sugars and glazes should go on doughnuts shortly after frying, while the doughnuts are still warm. Fillings, custards, and thicker icings should wait until doughnuts have cooled to room temperature. For a thicker, smoother glaze, try double-dipping. Dip the doughnut into the glaze once, then let it set and dry. Once the glaze has dried, dip again. If you're adding sprinkles, cereal, or candies to the tops of your doughnuts, add them before the glaze or icing has dried.

I ♥ NY

OLD-FASHIONED

JELLY

DOUBLE-DUTCH
CHOCOLATE

STRAWBERRY
AND CREAM

MARGARITA CAKE
WITH
TEQUILA GLAZE

--- PART 1 ---

UNITED STATES

CLASSIC AND CONTEMPORARY FAVORITES

From raised glazed jelly doughnuts to chocolate-sprinkled vanilla cake doughnuts, the United States is a country united in its love for doughnuts of all shapes, sizes, and flavors. Grown-ups dunk their doughnuts in a cup of coffee; kids wash theirs down with swigs of milk. They show up in convenience stores and supermarkets, in food trucks and farmers' markets, boxed up in huge industrial kitchens or fried all day long in brightly lit storefront doughnut shops. Even chain store doughnuts can inspire fierce loyalty through the nostalgia of childhood memory and regional identity.

Once, the richness of the doughnut—the sweetly spiced, eggy, fat-enriched dough, sometimes dotted with dried fruit or filled with custard or jam, the whole thing deep-fried to a golden brown, then lavished with icing or rolled in even more sugar and spice—made it a treat reserved for special occasions and particular holidays. But as the ingredients for doughnuts became cheaper and widely available, and as easy-to-use, fast-acting chemical rising agents like baking soda and baking powder replaced slower, fussier bread yeast, doughnuts became an everyday treat.

As diners, cafés, and luncheonettes spread across the country, so did the working man and woman's speedy, sugar-fueled breakfast: a cup of coffee and a doughnut, downed while perched on a vinyl stool alongside a metal-trimmed Formica counter. Diners courted local fame and drew customers even through blizzards by the excellence of their doughnuts. Much like pie, doughnuts inspired allegiance. A place had to be popular to earn a following for its doughnuts, since they were best eaten fresh. A hot doughnut was bliss; a stodgy day-old doughnut hardly worth the calories.

During World War I, a group of resourceful Salvation Army women, tasked with providing care and comfort to American soldiers in France, hit on the idea of making doughnuts. Frying doughnuts in rudimentary field kitchens under war-stressed conditions wasn't easy, but they did it, and soon the Salvation Army's "Doughnut Girls" were a resounding reminder of the comforts of home—or at least, a sweet, momentary respite from cold rations. The popular song "My Doughnut Girl" celebrated them; newsreels and newspapers showed off smiling lasses handing out doughnuts by the dozen to lines of men in uniform. Soldiers came home with a taste for doughnuts, and modern automation was there to fulfill it. What was once made by hand, dropped batch by batch into a kettle of boiling oil, was now fried by the dozen in automated machines that shaped, fried, and glazed while customers watched, enthralled, through bakery windows.

Cheap, sweet, and filling, the doughnut thrived during the Depression of the 1930s. As Sally Levitt Steinberg writes in *The Donut Book*, "In those days of breadlines, donuts became a staple of the working classes, a dozen in waxed paper for fifteen cents." Later, during World War II, the Red Cross followed the example of the Salvation Army, handing out thousands of doughnuts to soldiers near the front lines.

Doughnuts became, and remain, a great equalizer. Presidents and politicians eat them on glad-handing campaign stops, eager to show off their just-folks credentials. A generation of Cambodian refugees, fleeing the genocidal horrors of Pol Pot and his Khmer Rouge, supported themselves and their children by opening doughnut shops along the West Coast. As John T. Edge describes the process in *Donuts: An American Passion,* a new immigrant would go work for a family member's doughnut shop, then, with savings and loans from family and community, he'd open his own shop. One day's profit paid for the next day's bag of doughnut mix. Soon, as pointed out in the documentary film *Cambodian Doughnut Dreams,* 80 percent of the doughnut shops in Los Angeles were Cambodian-owned.

More and more, neighborhood doughnut shops may be using machines and mixes, but they still stand as sugar-scented community hubs, where for the price of a coffee and a doughnut anyone can find a welcome, and the kids who once jostled for just the right doughnut (extra sprinkles, please!) come back with their own kids in tow. Many small businesses, run by fine-dining pastry chefs or passionate self-taught bakers, are reviving made-from-scratch doughnuts, building their clientele with inventive, sometimes even zany, flavor palettes. These days, there are vegan doughnut shops, post-nightclub doughnut hangouts, doughnut carts, and doughnut trucks tracked on Twitter. The one thing we can be sure of? A doughnut may be a fleeting pleasure, but America's love affair with the doughnut is here to stay.

YEAST-RAISED DOUGHNUTS

MAKES 12 DOUGHNUTS AND 12 HOLES

The staple of every doughnut shop, the yeast-raised doughnut starts with nothing more than a light white bread dough enriched with butter and eggs. But given a crackly sheen of glaze or a thick swirl of icing, filled with custard, jelly, or cream, lavished with sprinkles or rolled in coconut, this sweet, airy doughnut can be transformed in dozens of ways. To make a tender doughnut, beware of overmixing or adding too much flour. The dough should be softer and more yielding than bread dough.

¾ cup warm milk (110° to 115°F)

1 package (2¼ teaspoons)
active dry yeast

2 large eggs

1 teaspoon vanilla extract

3 to 3½ cups unbleached
all-purpose flour

½ cup sugar

½ teaspoon salt

5 tablespoons unsalted butter, softened

Vegetable oil for deep-frying

1. Pour the warm milk into the bowl of a stand mixer fitted with a dough hook. Sprinkle the yeast over the milk and let stand for 5 minutes, then stir to dissolve the yeast.

2. Add the eggs and vanilla to the yeast mixture and beat on low speed for 1 minute.

3. In a medium bowl, combine 3 cups of the flour, the sugar, and salt. Stir with a whisk to blend. Add to the yeast mixture gradually and mix on low speed for 4 minutes, or until the dough begins to clear the sides of the mixer and form a ropy ball of dough around the hook.

4. With the machine running, add the butter, 1 tablespoon at a time, letting each piece be absorbed by the dough before adding the next. Continue mixing for 3 to 4 more minutes, adding the remaining ½ cup flour a little at a time as needed to make a soft dough.

5. Lightly oil a large bowl. Place the dough in the bowl and turn the dough to oil it. Cover with a damp clean kitchen towel or plastic wrap. Let the dough rise in a warm place for 1½ to 2 hours, or until doubled in bulk.

6. Punch the dough down gently. Lightly flour a work surface and a baking sheet. Turn the dough out onto the floured work surface. Using a rolling pin, roll the dough into a ½-inch-thick round. Using a doughnut cutter dipped in flour, cut out doughnuts and holes, flouring the cutter between each cut to prevent sticking. Arrange the doughnuts and holes on the floured baking sheet. Cover with a dry clean kitchen towel. Let rise for 45 to 60 minutes, or until the doughnuts are puffed.

7. In a Dutch oven or other deep, heavy pot, heat 2 to 3 inches oil over medium-high heat to 375°F on a candy or frying thermometer. Place a grid-patterned wire rack on a baking sheet, or line the pan with two layers of paper towels.

8. Using a slotted spoon or a skimmer, drop the doughnuts and holes into the hot oil in batches, being careful not to crowd the pan. Fry for 60 to 90 seconds per side, or until the doughnuts are golden brown and cooked through. (Doughnut holes should take 30 to 60 seconds per side.) Break open a "test doughnut" from the first batch to make sure the doughnuts are cooking correctly; adjust the heat level of the oil as needed.

9. Using a slotted spoon or a skimmer, transfer the doughnuts and holes to the wire rack or paper towels to drain.

GLAZED DOUGHNUTS

MAKES 12 DOUGHNUTS AND 12 HOLES

A thin glaze, made of powdered sugar and water with a touch of honey and vanilla, adds a crackled sweet coating to these classic doughnuts. If the glaze is your favorite part, give your doughnut a double dip.

VANILLA GLAZE

1¼ cups powdered sugar, sifted

2 teaspoons honey

Pinch of salt

1 teaspoon vanilla extract

2 tablespoons whole milk,
or more as needed

Yeast-Raised Doughnuts (page 30)

1. FOR THE GLAZE: In a medium bowl, combine the glaze ingredients and whisk until smooth, adding additional milk as needed if the glaze seems too thick. Dip the warm doughnuts into the glaze to cover both sides. Using tongs, place on a grid-patterned wire rack set on a baking sheet to let the glaze set for 10 minutes before serving. If desired, gently warm the glaze and give the doughnuts a second dip. Let the second coat set for a few minutes before serving.

JELLY DOUGHNUTS

MAKES 16 DOUGHNUTS

Here's the classic all-American jelly doughnut, which also happens to resemble, very strongly, the many jelly- and jam-filled doughnuts of Germany, Austria, and Central Europe. This method calls for sandwiching the jelly between two gently stretched rounds of dough, then frying the whole package. However, you can also fry simple rounds of plain dough and squirt in the jelly filling afterward using a pastry bag fitted with a plain tip.

You can make Sweetheat Doughnuts for Valentine's Day by using a heart-shaped cookie cutter. To finish, add a few drops of red food coloring to Vanilla Glaze (page 32), then sprinkle with chocolate or multicolored sprinkles.

Dough for Yeast-Raised Doughnuts (page 30), made through the first rise

¾ cup jam or jelly

Vegetable oil for deep-frying

Powdered sugar for dusting

1. Gently punch the dough down. Lightly flour a work surface and a baking sheet. Turn the dough out onto the floured work surface. Using a rolling pin, roll the dough into a ½-inch-thick round. Using a 2-inch biscuit cutter dipped in flour, cut out rounds of dough, flouring the cutter between each cut to prevent sticking. Stretch one round gently and mound 1 teaspoonful of jelly or jam in the center. Stretch another round and press it over the jam-topped round, pinching the edges together firmly. Repeat with the remaining rounds.

CONTINUED ·············→

2. Using 2½-inch biscuit cutter, cut off the excess dough from the edges of each round, rotating the cutter to seal the edges. Transfer the doughnuts to a lightly floured baking sheet, cover with a dry clean kitchen towel, and let rise in a warm place for 45 minutes, or until puffy.

3. In a Dutch oven or other deep, heavy pot, heat 2 to 3 inches oil over medium-high heat to 375°F on a candy or frying thermometer. Place a grid-patterned wire rack on a baking sheet, or line the pan with two layers of paper towels.

4. Using a slotted spoon or a skimmer, drop the doughnuts and holes into the hot oil in batches, being careful not to crowd the pan. Fry for 1 to 2 minutes on each side, or until the doughnuts are puffed, golden brown, and cooked through. Break open a "test doughnut" from the first batch to make sure the doughnuts are cooking correctly; adjust the heat level of the oil as needed.

5. Using a slotted spoon or a skimmer, transfer the doughnuts to the wire rack or paper towels to drain. Let cool.

6. Just before serving, sift powdered sugar over both sides of the doughnuts.

STRAWBERRY AND CREAM DOUGHNUTS

MAKES 16 DOUGHNUTS

Move over, strawberry shortcake! For this summertime treat, yeasted doughnuts are split open and filled with sweetened ripe strawberries and freshly whipped cream.

Dough for Yeast-Raised Doughnuts (page 30), made through the first rise

Vegetable oil for deep-frying

1 pint strawberries, hulled and thinly sliced

2 tablespoons plus 1 teaspoon granulated sugar

1 cup heavy cream

½ teaspoon vanilla extract

Powdered sugar for dusting

1. Gently punch the dough down. Lightly flour a work surface and a baking sheet. Turn the dough out onto the floured work surface. Using a rolling pin, roll the dough into a ½-inch-thick round. Using a 2½-inch biscuit cutter dipped in flour, cut out rounds of dough, flouring the cutter between each cut to prevent sticking.

2. Transfer the doughnuts to a lightly floured baking sheet, cover with a dry clean kitchen towel, and let rise in a warm place for 45 minutes or until the doughnuts are puffed.

3. In a Dutch oven or other deep, heavy pot, heat 2 to 3 inches oil over medium-high heat to 375°F on a candy or frying thermometer. Place a grid-patterned wire rack on a baking sheet, or line the pan with two layers of paper towels.

4. Using a slotted spoon or a skimmer, drop the doughnuts into the hot oil in batches, being careful not to crowd the pan. Fry for 1 to 2 minutes, then flip and fry for another 1 to 2 minutes, or until the doughnuts are puffed, golden brown, and cooked through. Break open a "test doughnut" from the first batch to make sure the doughnuts are cooking correctly; adjust the heat level of the oil as needed.

5. Using a slotted spoon or a skimmer, transfer the doughnuts to the wire rack or paper towels to drain. Let cool.

6. In a medium bowl, toss the strawberries with the 2 tablespoons sugar and let stand for 5 minutes, stirring occasionally, until the sugar is dissolved.

7. In a deep medium bowl, using a whisk or a hand-held electric mixer, beat the cream until thickened. Add the 1 teaspoon sugar and vanilla and continue beating until soft peaks form. Spoon into a pastry bag fitted with a ½-inch star tip.

8. Slice each doughnut horizontally, cutting about three-quarters of the way through. Gently pry open the doughnut and tuck in a layer of strawberries. Pipe in a thick ribbon of whipped cream. Repeat with the remaining doughnuts. Dust the doughnuts with powdered sugar and serve immediately.

VANILLA CAKE DOUGHNUTS

MAKES 12 DOUGHNUTS AND 12 HOLES

Forget race, religion, and politics: for doughnut lovers, there's only one real question: ARE YOU
A CAKE PERSON OR A YEAST-RAISED PERSON? *Of course, some doughnut fans will devour
any doughnut that comes their way, but even such omnivores will admit to a particular yen for
a chocolate-iced cake or a warm glazed. So for all of you who fall in the cakey camp, here's the
sweet, vanilla-scented classic. Dress it up, spice it up, or just enjoy it in all its pristine, child-
hood-invoking glory.*

*A fun idea if you're making doughnuts with kids: put the powdered or granulated sugar for
coating in a brown paper lunch bag. Add the finished doughnuts, a few at a time, close the bag,
and let the kids shake them in the sugar to coat.*

1¾ cups unbleached
all-purpose flour

1 teaspoon baking powder

½ teaspoon baking soda

¾ teaspoon salt

½ teaspoon freshly grated
nutmeg (optional)

2 tablespoons unsalted
butter, softened

½ cup granulated sugar

1 large egg

⅓ cup buttermilk

½ teaspoon vanilla extract

Vegetable oil for
deep-frying

Powdered sugar or
granulated sugar for
coating

1. Sift the flour, baking powder, baking soda,
salt, and nutmeg (if using) into a large bowl.

2. Using a hand-held electric mixer or stand
mixer, beat the butter and ½ cup granulated
sugar together. Beat in the egg. Add the buttermilk and vanilla and beat until the mixture is
smooth.

3. Add the flour mixture and mix on low speed until just combined, stopping once or twice to scrape down the sides of the bowl with a rubber spatula. If the dough seems very sticky, cover and refrigerate for up to 1 hour.

4. Lightly flour a work surface and a baking sheet. Place a grid-patterned wire rack on another baking sheet, or line the pan with two layers of paper towels.

5. Turn the dough out onto the floured work surface. Using a rolling pin, roll out the dough into a ½-inch-thick round. Dip a doughnut cutter in flour and cut out rounds, flouring the cutter between each cut to keep it from sticking. Arrange the doughnuts and holes on the floured baking sheet.

6. In a Dutch oven or other deep, heavy pot, heat 2 to 3 inches oil over medium-high heat to 365°F on a candy or frying thermometer. Pour the powdered sugar into a wide, shallow bowl.

7. Using a slotted spoon or a skimmer, drop the doughnuts and holes into the hot oil in batches, being careful not to crowd the pan. Fry for 60 to 90 seconds per side, or until the doughnuts and holes are golden brown and cooked through. (Doughnut holes should take 30 to 60 seconds per side.) Break open a "test doughnut" from the first batch to make sure the doughnuts are cooking correctly; adjust the heat level of the oil as needed.

8. Using a slotted spoon or a skimmer, transfer the doughnuts and holes to the wire rack or paper towels to drain.

9. Roll the warm doughnuts and holes in the sugar.

CONTINUED --------→

Variations:

CINNAMON SUGAR CAKE DOUGHNUTS

Follow the recipe for Vanilla Cake Doughnuts, but add 1 teaspoon ground cinnamon to the sugar for coating and stir to blend. Roll the warm dough-nuts in the cinnamon sugar.

LEMON–POPPY SEED CAKE DOUGHNUTS

Follow the recipe for Vanilla Cake Doughnuts, but substitute 2 teaspoons grated lemon zest and ½ teaspoon lemon extract for the vanilla extract. Add 2 tablespoons poppy seeds to the buttermilk mixture before adding the flour. Fry as directed. In a small bowl, beat 1½ cups sifted powdered sugar with 3 tablespoons fresh lemon juice. Spread the glaze over the warm doughnuts. Let the glaze dry before serving.

MARGARITA CAKE DOUGHNUTS WITH TEQUILA GLAZE

Follow the recipe for Vanilla Cake Doughnuts, but substitute 1½ teaspoons grated lime zest for the vanilla extract. Fry as directed. In a small bowl, beat 1¼ cups sifted powdered sugar with 2 tablespoons fresh lime juice and 1 tablespoon tequila. Spread the glaze over the warm dough-nuts. While the glaze is still wet, sprinkle each doughnut with a pinch of large-crystal salt, such as Hawaiian pink salt, Malden salt, or coarse sea salt. Allow the glaze to dry.

CHOCOLATE-GLAZED CAKE DOUGHNUTS

MAKES 12 DOUGHNUTS AND 12 DOUGHNUT HOLES

Dress up your vanilla cake doughnuts with a dunk in rich chocolate glaze to make this classic, kid-pleasing variation.

CHOCOLATE GLAZE

1¼ cups powdered sugar

3 tablespoons unsweetened cocoa powder

1½ tablespoons whole milk

1 teaspoon vanilla extract

Freshly made warm Vanilla Cake Doughnuts (page 38)

1. FOR THE GLAZE: Sift the sugar and cocoa together into a medium bowl. Add the milk and vanilla and stir until smooth.

2. In a small saucepan, warm the glaze over low heat. Using an icing spatula, spread the glaze over the top of the warm doughnuts. Let the glaze cool and set, then serve.

BIRTHDAY MINI-DOUGHNUT PYRAMID

MAKES 1 DOUGHNUT PYRAMID; SERVES 10 TO 12

Make a special day even sweeter with a birthday pyramid of glazed mini-doughnuts lit up with candles. For the prettiest presentation, use long, slender, French-style birthday candles, found in cookware stores.

Dough for Vanilla Cake Doughnuts (page 38), prepared through Step 3

Vegetable oil for deep-frying

Vanilla Glaze (page 32)

Chocolate Glaze (page 42)

Sprinkles

1. Lightly flour a work surface and a baking sheet. Place a grid-patterned wire rack on another baking sheet, or line the pan with two layers of paper towels.

2. Turn the dough out onto the floured work surface. Using a rolling pin, roll the dough into a ½-inch-thick round. Dip a 1½-inch biscuit cutter in flour and cut out rounds, flouring the cutter between each cut to keep it from sticking. Using the tip of a chopstick or the handle of a wooden spoon, poke a hole in the center of each doughnut. Arrange the doughnuts on the floured baking sheet.

CONTINUED ------------>

3. In a Dutch oven or other deep, heavy pot, heat 2 to 3 inches oil over medium-high heat to 365°F on a candy or fryer thermometer.

4. Using a slotted spoon or a skimmer, drop the doughnuts into the hot oil in batches, being careful not to crowd the pan. Fry for 60 to 90 seconds per side, or until the doughnuts are golden brown and cooked through. Break open a "test doughnut" from the first batch to make sure the doughnuts are cooking correctly; adjust the heat level of the oil as needed.

5. Using a slotted spoon or a skimmer, transfer the doughnuts and holes to the wire rack or paper towels to drain.

6. Dip half of the warm doughnuts in the vanilla glaze and the other half in the chocolate glaze. Top with sprinkles while the glaze is still wet. Allow the glaze to set and dry.

7. Arrange the doughnuts in concentric circles, each smaller than the last, to form a round pyramid. Slip a long birthday candle in the hole of each doughnut, and light just before serving.

OLD-FASHIONED DOUGHNUTS

MAKES 12 DOUGHNUTS AND 12 HOLES

In the world of doughnuts, the old-fashioned doughnut is distinguished from the cake doughnut by its craggy, "exploded" exterior. Those humps and ridges add textural interest and a higher proportion of crunchy fried outside to delicate-crumbed inside. To make the doughnuts crack and expand on contact with the hot oil, the dough needs more leavening, plus a little more fat to keep it tender. Baking soda plus sour cream makes this an old fashion worth reviving.

2½ cups unbleached all-purpose flour

2 teaspoons baking soda

½ teaspoon ground mace or freshly grated nutmeg

¼ teaspoon salt

¾ cup sugar

½ cup sour cream

2 large eggs

½ teaspoon vanilla extract

2 tablespoons unsalted butter, cut into bits and softened

Vanilla Glaze (page 32) (optional)

Vegetable oil for deep-frying

1. Sift the flour, baking soda, mace, and salt together into a large bowl. Make a well in the center of the mixture.

2. In a medium bowl, beat the sugar, sour cream, eggs, and vanilla together. Pour the egg mixture into the flour and mix gently, pulling in flour from the sides of the bowl to make a smooth dough. Stir in the butter until smooth. Cover and refrigerate for 20 minutes.

CONTINUED ------------>

3. Meanwhile, lightly flour a work surface and a baking sheet. Place a grid-patterned wire rack on another baking sheet, or line the pan with two layers of paper towels. If using the glaze, pour it into a wide, shallow bowl.

4. In a Dutch oven or other deep, heavy pot, heat 2 to 3 inches oil over medium-high heat to 365°F on a candy or frying thermometer.

5. Turn the dough out onto the floured work surface. Using a rolling pin, roll the dough into a ½-inch-thick round. Using a doughnut cutter dipped in flour, cut out doughnuts and holes, flouring the cutter between each cut to prevent sticking. Arrange the doughnuts and holes on the floured pan.

6. Using a slotted spoon or a skimmer, drop the doughnuts and holes into the hot oil in batches, being careful not crowd the pan. Fry for 60 to 90 seconds per side, or until the doughnuts and holes are golden brown and cooked through. (Doughnut holes should take 30 to 60 seconds per side.) Break open a "test doughnut" from

the first batch to make sure the doughnuts are cooking correctly; adjust the heat level of the oil as needed. Using a slotted spoon or a skimmer, transfer the doughnuts and holes to the wire rack or paper towels to drain and cool slightly.

7. When the doughnuts are cool enough to handle, dip them into the glaze. Arrange the doughnuts, glazed side up, on the wire rack to let the glaze cool and set. If desired, redip in the glaze for a second coat.

CHOCOLATE CAKE DOUGHNUTS

MAKES 12 DOUGHNUTS AND 12 HOLES

Most chain-store chocolate doughnuts don't use enough of the good stuff to come close to sating a true chocoholic's cravings. Here's the answer to your deepest cocoa-scented dreams. The secret? Using a high-quality Dutch-processed cocoa, which makes a darker, more deeply chocolaty doughnut. (Droste and Valrhona are two brands worth seeking out.) Patting out the rather sticky dough between two sheets of waxed paper or parchment paper, then chilling it for an hour or so before you start cutting and frying helps keep the dough from sticking to your hands, the work surface, and your cutter. Remember, moist doughs make tender doughnuts, so resist the urge to flour your dough into submission.

2 cups unbleached all-purpose flour

½ cup unsweetened cocoa powder, preferably Dutch processed

1 teaspoon baking powder

½ teaspoon salt

2 tablespoons unsalted butter, softened

½ cup plus 1 tablespoon granulated sugar

2 large egg yolks

1 teaspoon vanilla extract

⅔ cup whole milk

Vegetable oil for deep-frying

Granulated sugar for sprinkling or powdered sugar for dusting (optional)

1. Sift the flour, cocoa, baking powder, and salt together into a medium bowl.

2. In a large bowl using a hand-held electric beater or the bowl of a stand mixer fitted with the paddle attachment, beat the butter and sugar together. Beat in the egg yolks, one at a time. Beat in the vanilla extract.

PG. 47

CONTINUED

3. On low speed, add the flour in three increments, alternating with the milk, until just combined. Cover and refrigerate for at least 20 minutes or up to 1 hour.

4. In a Dutch oven or other deep, heavy pot, heat 2 to 3 inches oil over medium-high heat to 365°F on a candy or frying thermometer.

5. While the oil is heating, lightly flour a work surface and a baking sheet. Place a grid-patterned wire rack on another baking sheet, or line the pan with two layers of paper towels.

6. Turn the dough out onto the floured work surface. Using a rolling pin, roll the dough into a ½-inch-thick round. Using a doughnut cutter dipped in flour, cut out doughnuts and holes, flouring the cutter between each cut to prevent sticking. Place the doughnuts and holes on the floured pan.

7. Using a slotted spoon or a skimmer, drop the doughnuts and holes into the hot oil in batches, being careful not crowd the pan. Fry for 1 to 2 minutes per side, or until firm and cooked through. (Doughnut holes should take 30 to 60 seconds per side.) Using a slotted spoon or a skimmer, transfer the doughnuts and holes to the wire rack or paper towels to drain.

8. If desired, sprinkle the warm doughnuts and holes with granulated or powdered sugar.

Variation:

DOUBLE-DUTCH CHOCOLATE DOUGHNUTS

Add ⅓ cup (2 ounces) finely chopped bittersweet or semisweet chocolate to the dough before chilling.

GLUTEN-FREE
BAKED DOUBLE-CHOCOLATE DOUGHNUTS

MAKES 12 DOUGHNUTS

Since gluten-free doughnuts tend to be more tender and crumbly than those made with wheat flour, you'll have more luck keeping your doughnuts together if you bake them in a doughnut pan instead of frying them. Xanthan gum is a white powder that helps the dough cohere; look for it in natural foods or specialty foods stores.

¾ cup unsweetened cocoa powder

1½ cups hot water

1½ cups gluten-free flour mix (see note, page 50)

1 cup sugar

1½ teaspoons baking powder

1¼ teaspoons xanthan gum

½ teaspoon salt

½ teaspoon baking soda

2 large eggs, beaten

5 tablespoons canola oil, coconut oil, or melted butter

6 ounces bittersweet or semisweet chocolate chips

Powdered sugar for dusting (optional)

1. Preheat the oven to 350°F. Lightly butter a 12-ring doughnut pan.

2. In a large bowl, whisk the cocoa powder into the hot water until dissolved. Let cool to room temperature.

3. Sift the flour, sugar, baking powder, xanthan gum, salt, and baking soda together into a medium bowl.

CONTINUED ------------→

4. Beat the eggs and canola oil into the cocoa mixture. Stir in the flour mixture until blended, then stir in the chocolate chips. Pour the batter into the prepared pan, using about ¼ cup batter for each doughnut.

5. Bake for 16 to 18 minutes, or until the dough-nuts have risen and a cake tester inserted into a doughnut ring comes out clean. Unmold and serve warm. If desired, dust with powdered sugar before serving.

NOTE: Made from white and brown rice flour, tapioca flour, and potato starch, King Arthur's Gluten-Free Multi-Purpose Flour is our favorite gluten-free baking flour. However, you can also make your own gluten-free flour mix: for 1-1/2 cups of flour, combine 1 cup sweet brown or white rice flour, 1/4 cup tapioca flour, 2 tablespoons potato starch, and 2 tablespoons sweet sorghum flour in a bowl and stir with a whisk to blend.

MOLASSES SPICE

DOUGHNUT
MUFFINS

BOSTON CREAM

SOPAPILLAS

CALAS

MALASADAS

--- PART 2 ---

UNITED STATES

REGIONAL FAVORITES

Doughnuts came to America through many cultures. Dutch settlers in New Amsterdam brought their deep-fried olykoeks; by the time the city became Manhattan, the deep-fried sweet dough cakes were part of the city's gastronomic heritage. Beignets from France found a home in Francophone New Orleans; immigrants from the Azores introduced the Portuguese malasada, a pre-Lenten tradition, to the South Pacific shores of Hawaii.

Boston cream pie, a custard-filled, chocolate-topped cake created at Boston's Parker House Hotel, became the Boston cream doughnut, beloved far beyond its New England home. German immigrants brought their jelly-filled, sugar-dusted yeast-raised doughnuts to the prairie states of the upper Midwest; soon, the jelly doughnut was as American as apple pie.

APPLE CIDER DOUGHNUTS

MAKES 12 DOUGHNUTS AND 12 HOLES

Come autumn, farm stands offer not just apples but newly pressed apple cider, homemade apple pies, and irresistible freshly made apple cider doughnuts. Behind the counter, old-fashioned doughnut machines plop rings of batter into simmering oil. The doughnuts float down a canal of hot oil, flip over, and finally tumble down a chute under a snowfall of gritty cinnamon sugar. If you like a crunchy coating on your doughnuts, roll them in granulated sugar; for a softer, thicker dusting, use powdered sugar.

2 cups unbleached all-purpose flour

½ teaspoon freshly grated nutmeg

Pinch of ground allspice

½ teaspoon baking powder

¼ teaspoon baking soda

¼ teaspoon salt

1 large egg

1 large egg yolk

½ cup apple cider

2 tablespoons granulated sugar

3 tablespoons brown sugar

2 tablespoons unsalted butter, melted

Vegetable oil for deep-frying

CINNAMON SUGAR

½ cup granulated sugar or sifted powdered sugar

½ teaspoon ground cinnamon

1. Sift the flour, spices, baking powder, baking soda, and salt together into a large bowl. In a medium bowl, beat the egg, egg yolk, cider, and sugars together.

2. Stir the egg yolk mixture gently into the flour mixture to form a moist dough. Stir in the melted butter until just combined.

3. Lightly flour a work surface and a baking sheet. Transfer the dough to the floured work surface. Using a rolling pin, roll the dough into

CONTINUED -------------→

a ½-inch-thick round. Using a doughnut cutter dipped in flour, cut out doughnuts and holes, flouring the cutter between each cut to prevent sticking. Place the doughnuts and holes on the floured pan. Let rest for 10 minutes while the oil is heating.

4. In a Dutch oven or other deep, heavy pot, heat 2 to 3 inches oil over medium-high heat to 365°F on a candy or frying thermometer. Place a grid-patterned wire rack on a baking sheet, or line the pan with two layers of paper towels.

5. FOR THE CINNAMON SUGAR: Add the sugar and cinnamon to a brown paper lunch bag, then close the bag and shake it to mix the cinnamon sugar.

6. Using a slotted spoon or a skimmer, drop the doughnuts and holes into the hot oil in batches to avoid crowding the pan. Fry for 60 to 90 seconds on each side, or until golden brown and cooked through. (Doughnut holes should take 30 to 60 seconds per side.)

7. Using a slotted spoon or a skimmer, transfer the doughnuts and holes to the wire rack or paper towels to drain.

8. Working in batches, drop the warm doughnuts and holes into the bag of cinnamon sugar. Shake until the doughnuts and holes are coated. Transfer the sugared doughnuts and holes to a serving plate.

BOSTON CREAM DOUGHNUTS

MAKES 12 TO 14 DOUGHNUTS

When it comes to having fans in Massachusetts, the Boston cream doughnut is second only to the Red Sox. It's a one-handed version of Boston cream pie, which was invented in the 1850s at the city's venerable Parker House Hotel. Despite the name, Boston cream pie isn't a pie at all, but a custard-filled, chocolate-topped sponge cake. Reinvented as a fluffy yeast-raised doughnut bulging with rich vanilla custard and slicked with chocolate glaze, it became the official state doughnut of Massachusetts in 2003.

¾ cup warm milk
(110° to 115°F)

1 package (2¼ teaspoons)
active dry yeast

2 large eggs

1 teaspoon vanilla extract

3 to 3½ cups unbleached
all-purpose flour

½ cup sugar

½ teaspoon salt

5 tablespoons unsalted
butter, softened

Vegetable oil for deep-
frying

Vanilla Custard Filling
(recipe follows)

Chocolate Icing
(recipe follows)

1. Pour the warm milk into a large bowl, or into the bowl of a stand mixer fitted with a dough hook. Sprinkle the yeast over the milk and let stand for 5 minutes. Stir to dissolve the yeast.

2. Add the eggs and vanilla to the yeast mixture. Using a hand-held whisk or the dough hook, mix on low speed for 1 minute.

PG. 57

CONTINUED ------------>

3. Add 3 cups of the flour and the sugar and salt to the yeast mixture and beat with a wooden spoon or mix with the dough hook on low speed for 4 minutes, or until the dough begins to clear the sides of the bowl and form a ropy ball around the spoon or hook.

4. If mixing the dough by hand, beat in the butter 1 tablespoon at a time. If using a stand mixer, with the machine running, add the butter 1 tablespoon at a time, letting each piece be absorbed by the dough before adding the next. Continue mixing for 3 or 4 more minutes, adding the remaining ½ cup flour 1 tablespoonful at a time as needed to make a soft dough.

5. Lightly oil a large bowl. Put the dough in the bowl and turn to oil it. Cover with a damp clean kitchen towel and let rise in a warm place for 1½ to 2 hours, or until doubled in bulk.

6. Lightly flour a work surface and a baking sheet. Punch down the dough and turn it out onto the floured work surface. Using a rolling pin, roll the dough into a ½-inch-thick round. Using a 2½-inch biscuit cutter, cut out rounds, flouring the cutter between each cut to keep it from sticking.

7. Place the rounds on the floured baking sheet. Cover with a dry clean kitchen towel. Let rise for 45 to 60 minutes, or until the rounds are puffed and nearly doubled in size.

8. In a Dutch oven or other deep, heavy pot, heat 2 to 3 inches oil over medium-high heat to 365°F on a candy or frying thermometer. Place a grid-patterned wire rack on a baking sheet, or line the pan with two layers of paper towels.

9. Using a slotted spoon or a skimmer, drop the rounds into the hot oil in batches, being careful not to crowd the pan. Fry for about 1 minute, then flip over and continue frying for another 1 to 2 minutes, or until the doughnuts are golden brown and cooked through. Break open a "test dough-nut" from the first batch to make sure they are cooking evenly; adjust heat as needed if dough-nuts are browning too fast. Using a slotted spoon or a skimmer, transfer to the wire rack or paper towels to drain and cool to room temperature.

10. To assemble, spoon the vanilla custard into a pastry bag fitted with a plain tip. Using a small, sharp knife or the end of a chopstick, make a hole in the side of a doughnut.

11. Insert the tip of the pastry bag into the hole and squeeze a dollop of cream into each doughnut, using about 1 rounded teaspoon of filling per doughnut, or until the doughnut plumps up in a pleasing way. Repeat with all the remaining doughnuts.

12. Using an icing spatula or a butter knife, spread an even layer of warm icing over the top of each doughnut. Let the icing cool and set.

13. If not serving immediately, cover and refrigerate the doughnuts until serving. These doughnuts are best served within a few hours of frying.

VANILLA CUSTARD FILLING

MAKES 2½ CUPS

2 cups whole milk or half-and-half
1 vanilla bean, split lengthwise, or 1 tablespoon vanilla extract
6 large egg yolks
½ cup sugar
3 tablespoons cornstarch
2 tablespoons unsalted butter

1. In a small saucepan, heat the milk over medium-low heat until small bubbles form around the edges of the pan. Add the vanilla bean, if using. Cover and let steep for 10 minutes. Scrape the seeds out of vanilla pod halves into the milk, using the tip of a small paring knife. Discard the pod halves. Gently reheat the milk again.

2. In a medium bowl, whisk the egg yolks briefly. Add the sugar and cornstarch and beat until the mixture is smooth and thick. In a slow but steady stream, gradually whisk in the hot milk, whisking vigorously.

CONTINUED ------------>

3. Transfer the mixture to a heavy, medium saucepan. Cook over medium heat, whisking constantly, until the mixture begins to thicken, then reduce the heat and whisk until thickened and glossy.

4. Beat in the butter and vanilla extract, if using. Scoop into a bowl. Press plastic wrap directly onto the surface of the cream to prevent a skin from forming. Refrigerate for at least 2 hours or up to 3 days.

CHOCOLATE ICING

MAKES 1 CUP

¼ cup heavy cream or half-and-half, warmed

6 ounces bittersweet or semisweet chocolate chips

1. In a medium bowl, pour the cream over the chocolate pieces. Stir until the chocolate is melted and smooth. If necessary, set the bowl over a saucepan of simmering water until the chocolate is melted, or microwave the mixture in 10-second increments, stirring well after each time, and being careful not to scorch the chocolate.

2. Use now, or reheat gently to use later.

DOUGHNUT MUFFINS

MAKES 12 MUFFINS

Want to scratch that doughnut itch without getting out the fryer? The Downtown Bakery and Creamery in Healdsburg, California, makes a wide array of excellent baked goods, but Sonoma County locals know that nothing starts the day better than one of their fresh-out-of-the-oven doughnut muffins. The secret of the muffin-into-doughnut transformation? A post-bake dunk into melted butter, followed by an all-over dip in cinnamon sugar. This is our version of their popular muffin.

¾ cup (1½ sticks) unsalted butter, softened

¾ cup sugar

2 large eggs

3 cups unbleached all-purpose flour

2½ teaspoons baking powder

¼ teaspoon baking soda

½ teaspoon salt

1 teaspoon freshly grated nutmeg

½ cup milk

⅓ cup buttermilk or plain yogurt

CINNAMON SUGAR DIP

1 cup sugar

1 teaspoon ground cinnamon

½ cup (1 stick) unsalted butter, melted

1. Preheat the oven to 350°F. Butter and flour a 12-cup muffin pan, or line with paper liners.

2. In a large bowl using a hand-held electric mixer or in the bowl of a stand mixer fitted with the paddle attachment, cream the ¾ cup butter and the ¾ cup sugar until light and fluffy. Beat in the eggs one at a time.

3. Sift the flour, baking powder, baking soda, salt, and nutmeg together into a medium bowl. In another bowl, stir the milk and buttermilk together.

PG. 61

CONTINUED ⇢

4. Gently stir one-third of the dry ingredients into the butter mixture. Follow with one-third of the milk mixture. Repeat, alternating dry and wet mixtures, until just combined.

5. Divide the batter among the muffin cups, using about 1½ cups per cup. Bake for 30 to 35 minutes, or until the muffins are golden brown and a cake tester inserted in the center of a muffin comes out clean. Let cool in the pan on a wire rack for 10 minutes.

6. FOR THE DIP: Combine the sugar and cinnamon in a small bowl and stir to blend. Remove a muffin from the pan and dip it in or brush it with the melted butter. Roll the top of the muffin in the cinnamon sugar. Repeat with the remaining muffins.

BEIGNETS

MAKES 16 BEIGNETS

As any resident can tell you, a good day in the Crescent City starts with hot beignets and strong coffee, even if you do have to brush a thick veil of powdered sugar off your shirt front afterward. And while a freshly made plain beignet is perfection in itself, many pastry chefs are now gilding the lily, by dressing up beignets and serving them for dessert, with fancy sauces.

1 package (2¼ teaspoons) active dry yeast

2 tablespoons warm water

4½ cups unbleached all-purpose flour

¼ cup granulated sugar

½ teaspoon salt

1 cup whole milk

4 tablespoons unsalted butter

1 large egg, beaten

Vegetable oil for deep-frying

Powdered sugar for dusting

1. In a small bowl, sprinkle the yeast over the warm water. Let stand for 5 minutes, then stir briefly to dissolve the yeast.

2. In a large bowl or the bowl of a stand mixer fitted with the paddle attachment, combine the flour, sugar, and salt. Stir with a whisk to blend, or mix briefly at low speed.

3. In a medium saucepan, heat the milk and butter over medium heat until the butter melts and small bubbles form around the edges of the pan. Pour the hot milk mixture into the flour mixture and beat briskly with a whisk or the stand mixer on medium-low speed until just mixed. Add the egg and the yeast mixture and beat vigorously until smooth.

PG. 65

CONTINUED

4. Cover the bowl with a damp clean towel or plastic wrap and let rise in a warm place for 45 to 60 minutes, or until doubled in size.

5. In a Dutch oven or other deep, heavy pot, heat 2 to 3 inches oil over medium-high heat to 365°F on a candy or frying thermometer. Place a grid-patterned wire rack on a baking sheet, or line the pan with two layers of paper towels. Preheat the oven to 250°F.

6. While the oil is heating, lightly flour a work surface and another baking sheet. Gently deflate the dough and turn it out on the floured surface. Using a rolling pin, roll the dough out into a ½-inch-thick rectangle. Using a sharp knife, cut the rectangle into 12 squares, each about 2 inches square. Arrange the squares on the floured baking sheet. Let rise for 15 to 20 minutes, or until gently puffed.

7. Using a slotted spoon or a skimmer, drop the beignets into the hot oil in batches to avoid crowding the pan. Fry for 60 to 90 seconds on each side, or until golden brown. Using a slotted spoon or a skimmer, transfer the beignets to the wire rack or paper towels to drain. Keep finished beignets warm in the oven while you fry the next batch.

8. Dust the beignets with powdered sugar and serve warm.

St. Charles streetcar, New Orleans, La., 1923

USA 20c

Variation:

BEIGNETS WITH CHOCOLATE RUM SAUCE

MAKES 16 BEIGNETS

A rum-spiked chocolate dipping sauce turns these beignets into a sophisticated dessert.

CHOCOLATE RUM SAUCE

9 ounces bittersweet or semisweet chocolate, chopped

3 tablespoons dark rum

1 tablespoon sugar, or to taste

1 cup half-and-half

1 teaspoon vanilla extract

Freshly made warm Beignets (page 65)

1. FOR THE RUM SAUCE: In a medium bowl, combine the chocolate, rum, and sugar.

2. In a small saucepan, heat the half-and-half over medium-low heat until small bubbles form around the edges of the pan. Pour over the chocolate and stir until the chocolate is melted and smooth. Stir in the vanilla. Taste for sweetness; add more sugar if necessary.

3. Serve the warm beignets drizzled with the chocolate sauce instead of powdered sugar. Save the remaining sauce for dipping.

CALAS

MAKES 12 CALAS

BELLES CALAS! BELLES CALAS! TOUTES CHAUDES! That was the cry heard early in the morning along the streets of the French Quarter in New Orleans during the late nineteenth and early twentieth centuries, as Creole women hawked baskets full of these hot, freshly fried rice balls. Once bought, the calas would be drenched in dark sugarcane syrup and served for breakfast alongside steaming café au lait. During the rising and frying process, most of the rice dissolves, leaving the finished fritters with an alluringly spongy texture.

3 cups water

½ cup long-grain white rice

1⅛ teaspoons active dry yeast

½ cup warm water (110° to 115°F)

¼ cup unbleached all-purpose flour

¼ teaspoon salt

¼ teaspoon freshly grated nutmeg

Pinch of ground cloves

3 large eggs

¼ cup packed light brown sugar

½ teaspoon grated lemon or orange zest (optional)

Vegetable oil for deep-frying

Powdered sugar for dusting or cane syrup for serving (see note)

1. In a small, heavy saucepan, bring the water to a boil and add the rice. Partially cover and simmer, stirring occasionally, until the rice is very soft, about 25 minutes.

2. Drain the rice and let cool. Transfer the rice to a large bowl and mash the rice with the back of a large spoon to make a coarse paste. Sprinkle the yeast over the warm water and let stand for 5 minutes. Stir to dissolve the yeast.

3. Pour the yeast mixture over the rice paste. Stir well, cover, and let stand for 6 to 8 hours or overnight.

4. Combine the flour, salt, and spices in a medium bowl and stir with a whisk to blend. Beat the eggs, brown sugar, and lemon zest, if using, into the rice mixture. Stir in the flour until blended. Cover the bowl and set aside in a warm spot for 30 minutes, or until the batter is light and bubbled on top.

5. In a Dutch oven or other deep, heavy pot, heat 2 to 3 inches oil over medium-high heat to 350°F on a candy or frying thermometer. Place a grid-patterned wire rack on a baking sheet, or line the pan with two layers of paper towels. Preheat the oven to 250°F.

6. Scoop up the rice batter by tablespoonfuls and drop them into the hot oil in batches, taking care to avoid crowding the pan. Fry until golden brown, about 3 minutes. The calas should flip over during frying; if not, nudge them over with a slotted spoon or a skimmer to cook on both sides.

7. Using a slotted spoon or a skimmer, transfer the calas to the wire rack or paper towels to drain. Keep finished calas warm in the oven while you fry the remaining batter.

8. Serve hot, dusted with powdered sugar or drizzled with warm cane syrup.

NOTE: Cane syrup is made from the juice of crushed sugarcane, boiled down into a syrup. Look for it in specialty foods stores or supermarkets with a Southern foods section. For the most authentic flavor, choose pure cane syrup, rather than a mixture of cane and corn syrup. Steen's 100% Pure Cane Syrup, packaged in a distinctive bright-yellow can, is a commonly available brand.

COCONUT CAKE DOUGHNUTS

MAKES 12 DOUGHNUTS AND 12 HOLES

Topped with feathery wisps of coconut nestled into thick swaths of white icing, coconut layer cakes are a staple at parties and bake sales all across the South. These coconut doughnuts are a tasty hand-held version. Want pretty pastels for an Easter party or bridal shower? Separate the coconut topping into several small bowls and color each one with a drop or two of food coloring.

1¾ cups unbleached all-purpose flour

1 teaspoon baking powder

½ teaspoon baking soda

¾ teaspoon salt

2 tablespoons coconut oil

½ cup sugar

1 large egg

⅓ cup buttermilk

½ teaspoon coconut extract

Vegetable oil for deep-frying

Vanilla Glaze (page 32)

1 cup sweetened shredded coconut

1. Sift the flour, baking powder, baking soda, and salt together into a large bowl or the bowl of a stand mixer fitted with the paddle attachment.

2. Using an electric mixer or the paddle attachment, beat the coconut oil and sugar together on low speed. Beat in the egg. Add the buttermilk and coconut extract and beat until smooth.

3. On low speed, beat in the flour mixture until blended. If the dough seems very sticky, cover and refrigerate for at least 15 minutes or up to 1 hour.

CONTINUED

4. Lightly flour a work surface and a baking sheet. Place a grid-patterned wire rack on another baking sheet, or line the pan with two layers of paper towels.

5. Turn the dough out onto the floured work surface. Using a rolling pin, roll the dough into a ½-inch-thick round. Dip a doughnut cutter in flour and cut out doughnuts and holes, flouring the cutter between each cut to keep it from sticking. Arrange the doughnuts and holes on the floured baking sheet. Pour the glaze into a wide, shallow bowl. Spread the coconut in another wide, shallow bowl.

6. In a Dutch oven or other deep, heavy pot, heat 2 to 3 inches oil over medium-high heat to 365°F on a candy or frying thermometer.

7. Using a slotted spoon or a skimmer, drop the doughnuts and holes into the hot oil in batches, being careful not to crowd the pan. Fry for 60 to 90 seconds on each side, or until golden brown and cooked through. (Doughnut holes should take 30 to 60 seconds per side.)

8. Using slotted spoon or a skimmer, transfer the doughnuts and holes to the wire rack or paper towels to drain.

9. Dip the tops of the warm doughnuts and holes into the glaze. While the glaze is still wet, dip the glazed tops into the coconut, pressing the coconut into the glaze. Let the glaze dry and set before serving.

FUNNEL CAKES

MAKES 8 TO 10 FUNNEL CAKES, DEPENDING ON SIZE

These free-form sugared squiggles have become synonymous with state fairs and carnivals across the country, but their heritage goes back to the German ancestry of the Amish and Mennonite communities in Pennsylvania and Ohio. You'll get the roundest, prettiest results if you drizzle your batter inside a funnel cake ring set in a deep skillet; you can also use the outside ring of a 6- to 8-inch springform pan. Use a funnel or squeeze bottle to pour your batter into the characteristic swirly rings.

2 cups unbleached all-purpose flour

1½ teaspoons baking powder

½ teaspoon ground cinnamon (optional)

¼ teaspoon salt

1½ cups whole milk

2 large eggs

⅓ cup packed light brown sugar

½ teaspoon vanilla extract

Vegetable oil for deep-frying

Powdered sugar for dusting

1. Sift the flour, baking powder, cinnamon, and salt together into a large bowl. In a medium bowl, beat the milk, eggs, brown sugar, and vanilla together until blended.

2. Whisk the egg mixture into the flour mixture to make a smooth batter.

3. Place a funnel-cake ring or the outside ring of a 6- to 8-inch springform pan into a 3-inch deep skillet. Heat 2 inches oil (ring should rise about ¼ to ½ inch above the level of the oil) over medium-high heat to 365°F on a candy or frying thermometer. Place a grid-patterned rack on a baking sheet, or line the pan with two layers of paper towels .

CONTINUED ------>

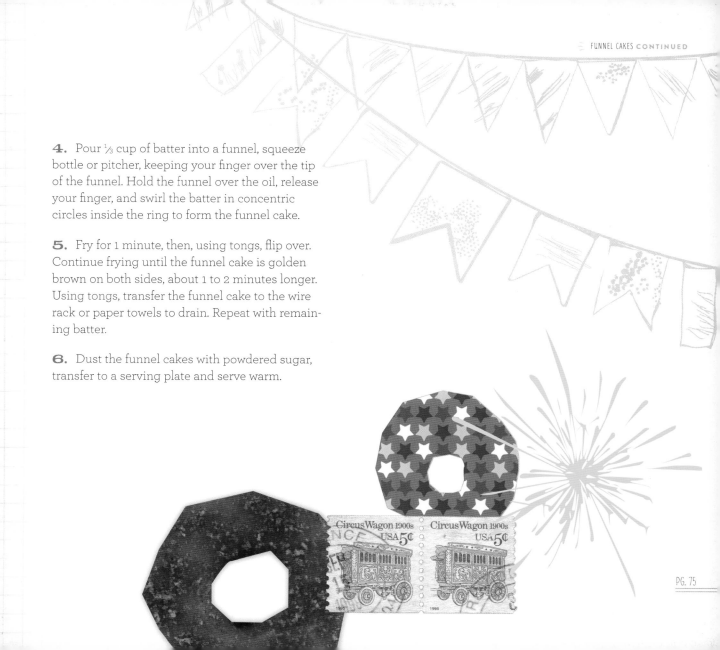

4. Pour ⅓ cup of batter into a funnel, squeeze bottle or pitcher, keeping your finger over the tip of the funnel. Hold the funnel over the oil, release your finger, and swirl the batter in concentric circles inside the ring to form the funnel cake.

5. Fry for 1 minute, then, using tongs, flip over. Continue frying until the funnel cake is golden brown on both sides, about 1 to 2 minutes longer. Using tongs, transfer the funnel cake to the wire rack or paper towels to drain. Repeat with remaining batter.

6. Dust the funnel cakes with powdered sugar, transfer to a serving plate and serve warm.

MOLASSES SPICE DOUGHNUTS

MAKES 12 DOUGHNUTS AND 12 HOLES

Why should cinnamon always get top billing at the doughnut shop? This doughnut is a spice-scented adaptation of the legendary doughnuts served at Zingerman's Bakehouse, a road trip-worthy bakery in Ann Arbor, Michigan. In a nod to the Upper Midwest's Scandinavian heritage, these doughnuts skip the cinnamon in favor of cardamom, whose lemony-herbal scent perfumes many Swedish, Norwegian, and Finnish pastries.

2½ cups unbleached all-purpose flour

1½ teaspoons baking powder

1 teaspoon freshly grated nutmeg

½ teaspoon ground ginger

½ teaspoon ground cardamom

¾ teaspoon salt

¼ cup buttermilk

1 large egg

1 large egg yolk

¼ cup plus 2 tablespoons granulated sugar

4 tablespoons unsalted butter, melted and cooled

2 tablespoons molasses

Vegetable oil for deep-frying

½ cup muscovado or turbinado sugar, for sprinkling (see note)

1. Sift the flour, baking powder, spices, and salt together into a large bowl. In a medium bowl, whisk the buttermilk, egg, egg yolk, granulated sugar, melted butter, and molasses together until blended.

2. Using a wooden spoon, gently stir the wet ingredients into the flour mixture until just combined. Cover the bowl and refrigerate for at least 1 hour or up to 4 hours.

3. In a Dutch oven or other deep, heavy pot, heat 2 to 3 inches oil over medium-high heat to 365°F on a candy or fryer thermometer.

4. While the oil is heating, lightly flour a work surface and a baking sheet. Place a grid-patterned wire rack on another baking sheet, or line the pan with two layers of paper towels. Fill a wide, shallow bowl with the muscovado sugar.

5. Turn the chilled dough out onto the floured work surface and knead gently four or five times. Using a rolling pin, roll the dough to a ½-inch-thick round. Dip a doughnut cutter in flour and cut out doughnuts and holes, flouring the cutter between each cut to prevent sticking. Arrange the doughnuts and holes on the floured pan.

6. Using a slotted spoon or a skimmer, drop doughnuts and holes into the hot oil in batches to avoid crowding the pan. Fry, flipping each doughnut twice, for 3 to 4 minutes (less for the holes), until the doughnuts and holes are golden brown and cooked through. Using a slotted spoon or a skimmer, transfer the doughnuts and holes to the wire rack or paper towels to drain and cool slightly.

7. Roll the warm doughnuts and holes in the sugar. Serve warm.

NOTE: If you can find muscovado sugar (a large-crystal, raw brown sugar with a rich caramelly taste), use it for rolling the finished doughnuts. Otherwise, turbinado, a large-crystal raw cane sugar, works well.

VEGAN PUMPKIN DOUGHNUT HOLES

MAKES 24 DOUGHNUT HOLES

Ground flaxseed meal helps these doughnuts hold together during frying, while pumpkin puree gives them moistness and an earthy autumn flavor that makes them a great addition to Halloween party menus. Since this recipe only calls for a small amount of flaxseed meal, you'll get the freshest results by buying whole flaxseeds and grinding them yourself in a spice grinder or mini-chopper.

1 tablespoon ground flaxseed

1½ tablespoons warm water

¼ cup almond milk

¼ cup apple-cider vinegar

1⅔ cups unbleached all-purpose flour

2 teaspoons baking powder

1 teaspoon baking soda

1 teaspoon ground cinnamon

½ teaspoon freshly grated nutmeg

¼ teaspoon ground ginger

½ cup granulated sugar

2 tablespoons coconut oil

½ cup pumpkin puree

CINNAMON SUGAR

½ teaspoon ground cinnamon

½ cup granulated or sifted powdered sugar

Vegetable oil for deep-frying

1. In a small bowl, stir the ground flaxseed and water together until blended. In another small bowl, stir the almond milk and vinegar together.

2. Sift the flour, baking powder, baking soda, and spices together into a medium bowl.

3. In the bowl of a stand mixer fitted with the paddle attachment, or in a large bowl using a hand-held electric mixer, beat the sugar and

CONTINUED ------------>

coconut oil together until fluffy. Add the flax-seed mixture and beat until smooth. Beat in the pumpkin.

4. In three increments, mix in the flour mixture, alternating with the almond milk, scraping down the sides of the bowl with a rubber spatula as necessary, just until the batter is smooth. Cover and refrigerate for 45 minutes.

5. While the batter is chilling, place a grid-patterned wire rack on a baking sheet, or line the pan with two layers of paper towels. Fill a wide, shallow bowl with the cinnamon and sugar and stir to blend.

6. In a Dutch oven or other deep, heavy pot, heat 2 to 3 inches oil over medium-high heat to 365°F on a candy or frying thermometer.

7. Scoop up tablespoonfuls of batter and carefully drop them into the hot oil in batches, taking care not to crowd the pan.

8. Fry the doughnut holes for 1 or 2 minutes, turning them as needed, until golden brown and cooked through. Using a slotted spoon or a skimmer, transfer the holes to the wire rack or paper towels to drain. Let cool briefly.

9. Roll the warm doughnut holes in the cinnamon sugar. Serve warm.

MAPLE-BACON DOUGHNUTS

MAKES 12 DOUGHNUTS

Bacon's not just for breakfast anymore, now that its signature smoky-meaty goodness is showing up as a flavoring for everything from vodka to lip balm. (Bacon jam? Bacon gum? Vegan-kosher-bacon-flavored salt? YES, YES, AND YES.*) So it didn't take long for artisan doughnut shops across the country to turn everyone's favorite pancake combo into a sweet and savory doughnut. But while most doughnut shops just slick a maple-flavored glaze and a couple strips of bacon on the top of a regular yeast-raised, custard-filled doughnut, this recipe is built for true hard-core bacon fans, with a sweet-salty filling of bacon-infused, maple-sweetened custard and a real maple syrup glaze.*

Dough for Yeast-Raised Doughnuts (page 30), made through first rise

Vegetable oil for deep-frying

MAPLE-BACON CUSTARD FILLING

4 strips bacon, diced

2 cups whole milk or half-and-half

6 large egg yolks

2 tablespoons pure maple syrup, preferably Grade B

3 tablespoons cornstarch

⅓ cup packed light brown sugar or maple sugar

1 tablespoon unsalted butter

MAPLE GLAZE

1½ cups powdered sugar, sifted

2 tablespoons pure maple syrup, preferably Grade B

1 or 2 tablespoons milk, as needed

12 strips bacon

1. For the doughnuts, gently punch the dough down. Lightly flour a work surface and a baking sheet. Turn the dough out onto the floured work surface. Using a rolling pin, roll the dough into a ½-inch-thick round. Using a 2-inch biscuit cutter, cut out rounds of dough, flouring the cutter between each cut to prevent sticking. Transfer the doughnuts to the lightly floured baking sheet, cover with a dry clean kitchen towel, and let rise in a warm place for 45 minutes.

CONTINUED ------------→

2. In a Dutch oven or other deep, heavy pot, heat 2 to 3 inches oil over medium-high heat to 375°F on a candy or frying thermometer. Place a grid-patterned wire rack on a baking sheet or line the pan with two layers of paper towels.

3. Using a slotted spoon or a skimmer, drop the doughnuts into the hot oil in batches, being careful not to crowd the pan. Fry for 1 to 2 minutes, then flip and fry for another 1 to 2 minutes, or until the doughnuts are puffed, golden brown, and cooked through. Break open a "test doughnut" from the first batch to make sure the doughnuts are cooking correctly; adjust the heat level of the oil as needed.

4. Using a slotted spoon or a skimmer, transfer the doughnuts to the wire rack or paper towels to drain. Let cool.

5. FOR THE FILLING: In a medium skillet over medium heat, cook the diced bacon, stirring frequently, until browned and crisp. Using a slotted spoon, transfer to a double thickness of paper towels to drain.

6. Add about two-thirds of the bacon to a medium saucepan. Reserve the remaining third to add to the finished custard. Add the milk and heat over medium-low heat until bubbles form around the edges of the pan. Cover and let steep for 10 minutes. Pour through a fine-meshed sieve into a bowl. Discard the bacon bits.

7. In a medium bowl, using a whisk or a hand-held electric mixer, beat the egg yolks with the maple syrup. Sift the cornstarch into the sugar. Beat the sugar and cornstarch into the egg yolks until smooth and thick. In a slow but steady stream, gradually whisk in the hot milk.

8. Transfer the mixture to a heavy, medium saucepan. Over medium heat, whisk vigorously until the mixture begins to thicken, then reduce the heat and continue whisking until the mixture is thick and glossy. Remove from the heat.

9. Beat the butter and the reserved bacon bits into the pastry cream. Scoop into a bowl. Press plastic wrap directly onto the surface of the pastry cream to prevent a skin from forming. Refrigerate for at least 2 hours, until thoroughly chilled, or up to 3 days.

10. FOR THE MAPLE GLAZE: In a medium bowl, stir the powdered sugar and maple syrup together until blended. Stir in milk as needed to make a thin, dippable glaze.

11. In a medium skillet, fry the bacon strips in batches over medium heat until crisp and browned, draining excess fat as necessary. Using a slotted spatula, transfer to a double layer of paper towels to drain.

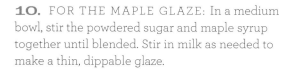

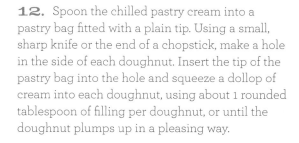

12. Spoon the chilled pastry cream into a pastry bag fitted with a plain tip. Using a small, sharp knife or the end of a chopstick, make a hole in the side of each doughnut. Insert the tip of the pastry bag into the hole and squeeze a dollop of cream into each doughnut, using about 1 rounded tablespoon of filling per doughnut, or until the doughnut plumps up in a pleasing way.

13. Using an icing spatula or a butter knife, spread an even layer of warm glaze over the top of each doughnut. Let the glaze cool and set, then spread another layer of glaze on top.

14. Break the cooked bacon strips in half. While the second layer of glaze is still wet, crisscross two half-strips of bacon on top of each doughnut. Let the glaze cool and set.

15. Serve now, or cover and refrigerate the doughnuts until serving. These doughnuts are best served within a few hours of frying.

SOPAPILLAS

MAKES 20 TO 24 SOPAPILLAS

SOAPYWHAT? Ask anyone born and raised in the Southwest, and you'll get nostalgic stories about these puffy, golden-brown triangles served every which way from Texas to New Mexico. Savory, they're a mop-up for meaty, chile-spiked stews; sweet, they're an anytime snack dusted in cinnamon sugar or dipped in honey or chocolate sauce. To be extra-authentic, serve them drizzled with mesquite or desert wildflower honey. Frying these in lard is traditional, but vegetable oil or shortening works just fine.

1½ cups warm water (110° to 115°F)

1 package (2¼ teaspoons) active dry yeast

1 tablespoon unsalted butter or lard, melted

1 tablespoon honey

3½ to 4 cups unbleached all-purpose flour

1 teaspoon salt

Vegetable oil or lard for deep-frying

Cinnamon Sugar (page 55) (optional)

½ cup honey, warmed

1. Pour the water into a large bowl. Sprinkle the yeast over the water and let stand for 5 minutes. Stir to dissolve the yeast.

2. Add the butter and honey to the yeast mixture. Stir the 3½ cups flour and the salt into the yeast mixture to form a soft dough.

3. Lightly sprinkle a work surface with flour. Turn the dough out and knead gently for 2 to 3 minutes, or until the dough is smooth and elastic. Add up to ½ cup more flour by the table-spoonful if the dough is very sticky; it should remain soft.

PG. 85

CONTINUED ------------→

4. Wash out the mixing bowl. Oil the bowl lightly and return the dough to the bowl, turning it to coat. Cover the bowl with a damp clean kitchen towel or plastic wrap and let rise in a warm place for about 1 hour, or until doubled in bulk.

5. In a Dutch oven or other deep, heavy pot, heat 2 to 3 inches oil over medium-high heat to 375°F on a candy or frying thermometer. If using, put the cinnamon sugar in a wide, shallow bowl.

6. While the oil is heating, punch down the dough. Lightly flour a work surface and a baking sheet. Place a grid-patterned wire rack on another baking sheet or line the pan with a double layer of paper towels. Turn the dough out onto the floured work surface. Using a rolling pin, roll the dough into a rectangle about ¼ inch thick. Using a sharp knife, cut the dough into 2- to 3-inch squares, then cut the squares in half on the diagonal to form triangles. Arrange the triangles on the floured pan.

7. Using a slotted spoon or a skimmer, drop the triangles into the oil a few at a time, being careful not to crowd the pan. They will sink, then float and puff up. After about 1 minute, flip them over to brown the other side for about 1 minute.

8. Using a slotted spoon or a skimmer, transfer the sopapillas to the wire rack or paper towels to drain. Roll the warm sopapillas in cinnamon sugar, if desired. Drizzle with honey and serve.

MALASADAS

MAKES 16 MALASADAS

Malasadas came to Hawaii with Portuguese immigrants from the Azores, a string of small volcanic islands off the Atlantic coast of Portugal, where these squares of fried sweet dough were served as part of Mardi Gras celebrations. Now, bakeries all across the islands serve these light, eggy treats as a delicious part of Hawaii's gastronomic history.

1 package (2¼ teaspoons) active dry yeast

¼ cup plus ⅓ cup warm water (110° to 115°F)

3 cups unbleached all-purpose flour

¼ cup granulated sugar

¼ teaspoon salt

3 large eggs, beaten

½ cup evaporated milk

2 tablespoons unsalted butter, melted

Vegetable oil for deep-frying

1 cup powdered sugar

1. In a small bowl, sprinkle the yeast over the ¼ cup warm water. Let stand for 5 minutes. Stir to dissolve the yeast.

2. In a large bowl, stir the flour, sugar, and salt together with a whisk. Make a well in the center of the flour mixture and pour in the eggs, evaporated milk, the ⅓ cup warm water, the melted butter, and the yeast mixture.

3. Stirring clockwise with a wooden spoon, gradually mix the flour mixture into the liquid ingredients to make a thick dough; it will be sticky. Cover with a damp clean kitchen towel and let rise in a warm place for 1 to 1½ hours, or until doubled in bulk.

PG. 87

CONTINUED ------------>

4. Punch down the dough. Lightly butter a baking sheet. Rub a small amount of butter or oil on your hands to prevent sticking. Pinch off a golf ball–sized piece of dough, flatten gently into a rough oval, and place on the buttered baking sheet. Repeat with the remaining dough. Cover with a dry clean kitchen towel and let rise for 15 minutes.

5. Meanwhile, in a Dutch oven or other deep, heavy pot, heat 2 to 3 inches oil over medium-high heat to 365°F on a candy or frying thermometer. Place a grid-patterned wire rack on a baking sheet, or line the pan with two layers of paper towels.

6. Using a slotted spoon or a skimmer, drop the malasadas into the hot oil in batches, being careful not to crowd the pan. Fry for 1 to 2 minutes, then flip to fry on the other side for another minute, until golden brown and cooked through but still moist inside. Using a slotted spoon or a skimmer, transfer to the wire rack or paper towels to drain. Let cool slightly.

7. Sift the powdered sugar over both sides of the warm malasadas until evenly coated. Transfer to a platter and serve warm.

Variation:

COCONUT MALASADAS

Replace the evaporated milk with an equal amount of coconut milk. Replace the butter with melted coconut oil. If desired, add ½ teaspoon coconut extract or 1 teaspoon coconut-flavored rum (such as Malibu) to the liquid ingredients before stirring them into the flour mixture.

CRAZY CRUNCH DOUGHNUTS

MAKES 10 DOUGHNUTS AND 10 HOLES

Remember how yummy that sugary, fake-fruit-flavored milk at the bottom of your bowl of Lucky Charms was? This doughnut takes three different crazy inspirations—the infused "cereal milk" used in desserts by New York City's Momofuku Milk Bar; candy-speckled Funfetti cake mix; and the sugary, kids'-cereal toppings used by Voodoo Doughnut in Portland, Oregon— and puts them all together into one wacky, crunchy, Homer Simpson-worthy doughnut.

½ **cup milk**

1 cup fruit-flavored cereal, like Froot Loops, Fruity Pebbles, or Lucky Charms

2 cups unbleached all-purpose flour

2 teaspoons baking powder

½ **teaspoon salt**

2 tablespoons unsalted butter, softened

¼ **cup sugar**

1 large egg

Vegetable oil for deep-frying

Vanilla Glaze (page 32)

1. In a small bowl, pour the milk over ¼ cup of the cereal and let stand for 10 minutes. When the cereal is soggy and the milk tastes sweet and fruity, pour the mixture through a sieve into a bowl. Reserve the milk and discard (or eat) the cereal.

2. Crush ¼ cup of the remaining dry cereal into coarse crumbs. Sift the flour, baking powder, and salt into a large bowl or the bowl of a stand mixer. Using a pastry cutter or the paddle attachment, cut or beat in the butter and crushed cereal until the mixture looks crumbly and sandy. Add the cereal milk, sugar, and egg and beat until blended. Cover and refrigerate the mixture for 30 minutes.

3. Meanwhile, in a Dutch oven or other deep, heavy pot, heat 2 to 3 inches oil over medium-high heat to 365°F on a candy or frying thermometer. Place a grid-patterned wire rack on a baking sheet, or line the pan with a double layer of paper towels. Pour the vanilla glaze into a wide, shallow bowl. Pour the remaining ½ cup cereal into another wide, shallow bowl.

4. Lightly flour a work surface and a baking sheet. Turn the dough out onto the floured work surface. Using a rolling pin, roll the dough into a ½-inch-thick round. Using a doughnut cutter dipped in flour, cut out doughnuts and holes, flouring the cutter between each cut to prevent sticking. Arrange the doughnuts and holes on the floured pan.

5. Using a slotted spoon or a skimmer, drop the doughnuts and holes into the hot oil in batches, being careful not to crowd the pan. Fry for 60 to 90 seconds on each side, until golden brown and cooked through. (Doughnut holes should take 30 to 60 seconds per side.) Using a slotted spoon or a skimmer, transfer the doughnuts and doughnut holes to the wire rack or paper towels to drain and cool slightly.

6. Dip the tops of the warm doughnuts and holes into the glaze. While the glaze is still wet, dip the glazed tops of the doughnuts and holes in the cereal. Let the glaze dry and set before serving.

BUÑUELOS

PICARONES

BOLINHOS

FILLED CHURROS

--- PART 3 ---

MEXICO AND SOUTH AMERICA

At Christmastime in Mexico, familes come together to eat, talk, and cook. Deft hands fold cornhusks or banana leaves around dozens and dozens of tamales ready for steaming. In another corner of the kitchen, a massive pillow of lard-enriched dough is kneaded and pounded, kneaded and pounded until it's stretchy and smooth. An hour of rest for the dough to relax, then egg-sized balls are pinched off and rolled, then flattened, pressed, and pulled into wide, flat circles the size of dinner plates. It takes adeptness and practice to make a perfectly even round without tearing, but with families and guests expecting to snack on fresh buñuelos throughout the holiday season, there's plenty of opportunity for novices to practice. Typically, once fried, buñuelos are broken into pieces and sprinkled with plain or cinnamon sugar. They can also be soaked in sugar syrup flavored with cinnamon, vanilla, or anise. To wash down the shattered crumbs, nothing else will do but a cup of thick Mexican hot chocolate, made with cakes of coarsely ground sweet chocolate flavored with almond and cinnamon.

This isn't the only type of buñuelo available in Mexico; in fact, there are many regional variations, some adding cheese, others using a richer, churro-like dough to make a soft, puffy round with a hole in the middle. But always, the buñuelos are dunked in sugar syrup, often a dark, rich version made from piloncillo, a mahogany-colored raw cane sugar sold in chunks or cones. And they're not just limited to the winter holidays; from saints' days to soccer matches, if a crowd is gathering, you won't have to look far to find a buñuelo stand.

What other fried treats are enjoyed in Mexico and beyond, to Central and South America? Churros, of course, very close to their Spanish counterparts, only these are frequently rolled in cinnamon sugar and filled with chocolate, vanilla pastry cream, eggy custard, or gooey dulce de leche. It's a pattern repeated throughout Central and South America, even the Caribbean, where pastries brought over by European colonizers have evolved to suit local ingredients and tastes. Pastes and preserves of aromatic tropical fruits, like guava, pineapple, and passion fruit, become the fruit fillings of choice, alternating with long-loved ingredients such as chocolate, coffee, coconut, and cinnamon. Dulce de leche, made from milk and sugar (or sweetened condensed milk) cooked down to a caramel, and cajeta, a similar product made from goat's milk, are used throughout Mexico; cajeta is also common in Argentina, where it's used as a filling for pastries and cookies. Fresh soft cheeses are beaten smooth with sugar and cinnamon, then used as fillings for freshly fried dough balls. The names are fanciful: in Brazil, two favorites are *sonhos* ("dreams"), and *bolinhos de chuva* ("rain cakes"), named for their raindrop shape.

Many of these fried treats are snacks enjoyed on the street, from small shops or sidewalk stalls that specialize in just one food. You may come to Peru to climb Machu Picchu, but you might leave with more memories of your favorite *picaroneria*, a small sidewalk stand or storefront specializing in Peruvian's favorite sweet snack, the squash-and-sweet-potato yeast-raised doughnuts known as picarones. Like buñuelos, picarones are also dunked after frying into a fragrant sugar syrup made from raw cane sugar, known locally as *chancaca*. Other treats are enjoyed in cafés and *panaderias*, or bakeries, where trays are heaped with baked and fried sweets in dozens of shapes, colors, and sizes. Served with hot chocolate or *café con leche*, these pastries add a welcome boost of sugar and spice to everyday life.

BUÑUELOS

MAKES 10 BUÑUELOS

Buñuelos, popular throughout Mexico, vary in style from region to region. This version, from Veracruz, uses a churro-like dough to make a puffy ring-shaped doughnut, flavored with aniseeds to give a hint of herbs and licorice. They can be enjoyed plain, but they're more often soaked in an anise-infused syrup made from piloncillo, the coarse dark brown raw sugar commonly used as a sweetener throughout Mexico. Lard would be the typical fat used for enriching the dough, but butter makes an acceptable (if not perfectly authentic) replacement.

SYRUP

One 8-ounce cone piloncillo, or 1 cup packed dark brown sugar

2 cups water

¼ teaspoon aniseeds

BUÑUELOS

1 cup water

3½ tablespoons lard or unsalted butter

¼ teaspoon aniseeds

¼ teaspoon salt

1¼ cups unbleached all-purpose flour

2 large eggs, beaten

¼ teaspoon baking powder

Vegetable oil for deep-frying

1. FOR THE SYRUP: Using the large holes of a box grater, shred the piloncillo into a medium saucepan. Add the water and aniseeds and bring to a simmer over medium-low heat, swirling the pan until the sugar has melted. Simmer for 15 to 20 minutes, swirling the pan occasionally, until reduced and thickened to a light syrup. Set aside.

2. FOR THE BUÑUELOS: In a medium saucepan, bring the water, lard, aniseeds, and salt to a boil over medium-high heat. Add the

CONTINUED ------>

flour all at once and cook, stirring vigorously with a wooden spoon, until the mixture pulls away from the sides of the pan and forms a ball. Remove from the heat.

3. Beat in the beaten eggs, about a tablespoon at a time, beating vigorously and making sure each addition is thoroughly absorbed before adding the next. Beat until the dough is smooth. You may not need all the eggs; stop when the dough can be gathered into a soft ball. Sprinkle the baking powder over the dough and mix in quickly and thoroughly.

4. In a Dutch oven or other deep, heavy pot, heat 2 to 3 inches oil over medium-high heat to 365°F on a candy or frying thermometer. Place a grid-patterned wire rack on a baking sheet, or line the pan with two layers of paper towels.

5. While the oil is heating, lightly flour a work surface or a baking sheet. Turn the dough out onto the floured work surface. Using a rolling pin, roll the dough into a ½-inch-thick round. Using a floured 2-inch biscuit cutter, cut out rounds, flouring the cutter between each cut to prevent sticking.

6. Using a slotted spoon or a skimmer, drop buñuelos in the oil in batches, being careful to avoid crowding the pan. Fry for 1 to 2 minutes on each side, or until golden brown and cooked through.

7. Using a slotted spoon or a skimmer, transfer to the wire rack or paper towels to drain. Just before serving, drizzle the syrup over the buñuelos. These are best served within an hour or two of frying.

Variation:

CINNAMON BUÑUELOS

Substitute one 4-inch stick cinnamon for the aniseeds in the sugar syrup. Replace the ¼ teaspoon aniseeds in the buñuelo dough with ¼ teaspoon ground cinnamon.

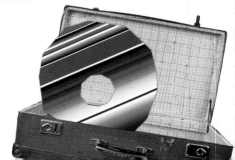

PICARONES

MAKES 12 PICARONES

Potatoes and sweet potatoes are both native to the Andean highlands of Peru, so it's no surprise that Peruvians created their own fried-dough treat to showcase the flavors of their homegrown produce. In Peru, raw dark brown cane sugar is called CHANCACA; *Mexican piloncillo, found at any market specializing in Latin American products, can be substituted, as can dark brown sugar.*

SYRUP

One 8-ounce cone piloncillo, or 1 cup packed dark brown sugar

2 cups water

2 cinnamon sticks

2 whole cloves

Stripped zest of 1 small orange

PICARONES

1 cinnamon stick

2 whole cloves

1 tablespoon aniseeds (optional)

6 cups water

8 ounces sweet potato, peeled and coarsely chopped (about 1 cup)

8 ounces butternut squash, peeled and coarsely chopped (about 1 cup)

2 packages (4½ teaspoons) active dry yeast

3 tablespoons sugar

¼ teaspoon salt

2 large eggs, lightly beaten

1¾ cups unbleached all-purpose flour

Vegetable oil for deep-frying

1. FOR THE SYRUP: Using the large holes of a box grater, shred the piloncillo cone into a medium saucepan or add the brown sugar. Add the water, cinnamon sticks, cloves, and orange zest and bring to a simmer, swirling the pan until the sugar has melted. Simmer for 15 to 20 minutes, swirling pan occasionally, until reduced and thickened to a light syrup. Set aside.

2. FOR THE PICARONES: In a medium saucepan, combine the cinnamon stick, cloves, aniseeds, if using, and water. Bring to a boil, reduce the heat to a simmer, and cook, partially covered, for 10 minutes. Strain out the spices

CONTINUED ------------→

and return the liquid to the pan. Add the sweet potato and squash, bring to a boil, reduce the heat to a simmer, and cook, partially covered, until the potato and squash are very tender, 15 to 20 minutes. Drain the potato and squash in a colander over a bowl, reserving 2 cups of cooking liquid.

3. Let the reserved cooking liquid cool to 110° to 115°F. Sprinkle the yeast into the cooking liquid and let stand for 5 minutes, then stir to dissolve the yeast.

4. In a stand mixer fitted with the paddle attachment, beat the potatoes and squash into a smooth puree. Beat in the sugar and salt, followed by the yeast mixture and the eggs, one at a time.

5. Switch to the dough hook. Add the flour in three increments, mixing well after each addition. On medium speed, mix the dough until it forms a soft, elastic dough, 4 to 6 minutes.

6. Transfer the dough to a lightly oiled bowl, turning to coat with oil. Cover with a damp clean kitchen towel or plastic wrap and let rise in a warm place for 1 hour, or until doubled in bulk.

7. In a Dutch oven or other deep, heavy pot, heat 2 to 3 inches oil over medium-high heat to 365°F on a candy or frying thermometer. Place a grid-patterned wire rack on a baking sheet, or line the pan with two layers of paper towels.

8. Gently punch the dough down. Using lightly greased hands, pinch off an egg-sized ball of dough, rolling it into a round. Push your thumb through the center of the ball to make a ring and drop the ring into the hot oil. Repeat with the remaining dough, working in batches and making sure not to crowd the pot.

9. Fry for 1 to 2 minutes on each side, or until the picarones are golden brown and cooked through. Using a slotted spoon or a skimmer, transfer to the rack or paper towels to drain.

10. Arrange warm picarones on a serving plate and drizzle with the syrup just before serving.

BOLINHOS DE CHUVA

MAKES 20 BOLINHOS

Known as "rain cakes" in Portuguese, these easy-to-make Brazilian doughnut balls get their name from their distinctive raindrop shape, made by scraping the soft batter off two spoons directly into hot oil. Sweet bolinhos are rolled in cinnamon sugar; savory ones leave out the sugar and add minced green onions to the batter. Using a mixture of flour and cornstarch makes for an extra-light and crispy doughnut.

2 large eggs

¼ cup sugar

1 teaspoon vanilla extract

1 cup unbleached all-purpose flour

½ cup cornstarch

2 teaspoons baking powder

Pinch of salt

½ cup whole milk

Vegetable oil for deep-frying

Cinnamon Sugar (page 55)

1. In the bowl of a stand mixer fitted with a paddle attachment or a medium bowl, combine the eggs and sugar. Using the stand mixer or a hand-held electric mixer, beat the eggs and sugar together on medium speed until light and fluffy, 1 to 2 minutes. Beat in the vanilla.

2. Sift the flour, cornstarch, baking powder, and salt into a medium bowl. On low speed, beat half the flour mixture into the egg mixture. Beat in the milk, followed by the remaining flour mixture. Beat until just combined.

CONTINUED ------------>

3. In a Dutch oven or other deep, heavy pot, heat 2 to 3 inches oil over medium-high heat to 350°F on a candy or frying thermometer. Place a grid-patterned wire rack on a baking sheet, or line the pan with two layers of paper towels. Put the cinnamon sugar in a wide, shallow bowl.

4. Dip 2 tablespoons briefly into the hot oil. Scoop up as much batter as you can hold in one spoon, then push it off into the hot oil with the other spoon. Repeat to cook the batter in batches, being careful to avoid crowding the pan. Fry for 3 to 4 minutes, turning as needed to ensure even browning, until the bolinhos are golden brown and cooked through but still moist inside.

5. Using a slotted spoon or a skimmer, transfer the bolinhos to the wire rack or paper towels to drain and cool slightly. Roll the bolinhos in the cinnamon sugar. Arrange on a serving plate and serve warm.

Variation:

SAVORY BOLINHOS

Follow the master recipe, deleting the ¼ cup sugar in the batter and increasing the salt to 1 teaspoon. Add ⅓ cup minced green onion to the batter and mix well. Fry as directed and serve plain.

SONHOS WITH GUAVA-CHEESE FILLING

MAKES 12 TO 14 SONHOS

Brazil is one of the world's largest guava producers, so ruby-red guava jelly, preserves, and pastes turn up as fillings in many different kinds of pastries. Here, guava paste and cream cheese, a common snack, is reinvented as a creamy, sweet-tart filling for sonhos, the popular Portuguese-style doughnuts. Queso fresco is a mild, spongy fresh cow's milk cheese; if you can't find it, substitute a mild feta cheese. Rinse the feta in several changes of fresh water to get rid of any excess salt.

FILLING

2 cups guava jelly or preserves

Grated zest and juice of 1 lime

Grated zest and juice of 1 small orange

One 4-ounce package cream cheese at room temperature

1 cup shredded queso fresco

⅓ cup sifted powdered sugar

SONHOS

1 teaspoon active dry yeast

2 tablespoons warm water

½ cup milk

¼ cup granulated sugar

2 tablespoons unsalted butter

½ teaspoon salt

2 cups unbleached all-purpose flour

1 large egg

Powdered sugar for dusting

1. FOR THE FILLING: In a small saucepan, combine the guava jelly with the zests and juices. Cook over medium heat for 1 minute, then remove from the heat and let cool.

2. In a medium bowl and using a hand-held electric mixer, beat the cream cheese on medium speed until fluffy. Beat in the shredded cheese and ⅓ cup powdered sugar. On low speed, gently mix in the guava jelly mixture until the filling is coarsely marbled red and white. Cover and refrigerate until needed.

CONTINUED ------------>

3. FOR THE SONHOS: In a small bowl, sprinkle the yeast over the warm water. Let stand for 5 minutes, then stir to dissolve the yeast.

4. In a medium saucepan, cook the milk over medium-low heat until bubbles form around the edges of the pan. Remove from heat and add the sugar, butter, and salt, stirring until the butter is melted.

5. Add the flour to the bowl of a stand mixer fitted with a dough hook. Make a well in the center of the flour. Add the milk mixture and beat on low speed. Add the yeast mixture and continue beating. Add the egg and increase the speed to medium. Continue beating until the dough is smooth, elastic, and pulls away from the sides of the bowl, 4 to 6 minutes.

6. Transfer the dough to a lightly oiled bowl. Turn the dough to coat it with oil. Cover with a damp clean kitchen towel or plastic wrap and let rise in a warm place for 1 hour, or until doubled in size.

7. Lightly flour a work surface and a baking sheet. Gently punch the dough down, transfer to the floured work surface, and divide into 12 to 14 pieces. Roll into balls about the size of a golf ball. Arrange on the floured pan, cover with a dry clean kitchen towel, and let rise again for 25 to 30 minutes, or until light and puffy.

8. In a Dutch oven or other deep, heavy pot, heat 2 to 3 inches oil over medium-high heat to 365°F on a candy or frying thermometer. Place a grid-patterned wire rack on a baking sheet, or line the pan with two layers of paper towels.

9. Using a slotted spoon or a skimmer, drop the balls into the hot oil in batches, being careful not to crowd the pan. Fry for 1 to 2 minutes on each side, or until the doughnuts are golden brown and cooked through. Using a slotted spoon or a skimmer, transfer to the wire rack or paper towels to drain and cool to room temperature.

10. Spoon the guava filling into a pastry bag fitted with a ½-inch plain tip. Using the end of a chopstick or the tip of a small, sharp knife, make a hole in the side of each doughnut. Insert the tip of the pastry bag and squeeze in a generous tablespoon of filling. Dust the doughnuts with powdered sugar. Arrange on a platter and serve.

FILLED CHURROS WITH MEXICAN HOT CHOCOLATE

MAKES 10 TO 12 CHURROS

The word churro got its name from a breed of Spanish sheep, the churra, which was the first breed brought to the New World by Spanish settlers in the sixteenth century. The curled, ridged curls of dough were thought to resemble the double pairs of curled horns on the heads of the churra rams. Born in Spain, this delectable breakfast treat is now found throughout Mexico as well as Argentina. It's almost always dunked in a cup of thick, cinnamon-scented hot chocolate. Professional churro-makers use a CHURRERA, *a long, thin, ridged tube with a wooden plunger for pushing the dough out into the bubbling oil, but you'll get very good results using a pastry bag fitted with a large star tip.*

1¼ cups dulce de leche (recipe follows)

Vanilla Custard Filling (page 59), or chocolate-almond or chocolate-hazelnut paste, such as Nutella

Churros (page 117)

Granulated sugar or Cinnamon Sugar (page 55), for rolling

1. Spoon the filling of your choice into a pastry bag fitted with a ¼-inch tip. Poke a metal or wooden skewer lengthwise through each churro to make a channel for the filling. Remove the skewer and insert the tip of the pastry bag in one end of the churro. Squeeze the bag to fill the churro. You may need to insert the tip of the pastry bag into the other end of the churro, squeezing to fill any remaining space. Repeat until all churros are filled.

2. Roll the filled churros in plain or cinnamon sugar before serving.

DULCE DE LECHE

MAKES 1¼ CUPS

If you can't find commercial dulce de leche, sold in Latino and specialty markets, you can make it yourself by cooking sweetened condensed milk down to a thick caramel syrup. Using a double boiler keeps the sugars from scorching during the cooking process.

One 14-ounce can sweetened condensed milk

1. Pour the milk into the top half of a double boiler. Fill the bottom half with several inches of water and bring to a simmer. Fit the top half of the double boiler over the simmering water.

2. Reduce the heat to medium-low and simmer gently for 1½ to 2 hours, adding more water to the double boiler as needed. Stir occasionally; the mixture is done when it has thickened and turned a deep golden brown.

3. Remove from the heat and pour into a container with a lid. Let cool, seal, and refrigerate. Dulce de leche will keep for several months.

CONTINUED ---------→

MEXICAN HOT CHOCOLATE

MAKES 4 SERVINGS

Abuelita ("grandmother") and Ibarra are two of the most common brands of Mexican drinking chocolate. Look for the cylindrical boxes, packed with individually wrapped tablets of chocolate scored into wedges. Coarse and grainy in texture, flavored with cinnamon and ground almonds, this chocolate is made to be melted into hot milk, then beaten to a froth using a whisk or a blender. If you can't find Mexican chocolate, use an equal amount of semisweet chocolate plus a generous pinch of cinnamon and a few drops of almond extract.

4 cups whole milk

6 ounces Mexican chocolate, broken into wedges or chunks

⅓ cup sugar, or to taste

1. SAUCEPAN METHOD: In a medium saucepan, heat the milk over medium-low heat until small bubbles form around the edges of the pan. Add the chocolate and heat, stirring, until the chocolate is melted. Taste and add sugar if needed. Remove from the heat and whisk vigorously until chocolate is emulsified and the mixture is frothy.

2. BLENDER METHOD: Heat the milk as above. Drop the chocolate pieces into a blender, then add the hot milk. Cover and blend on medium speed for 30 seconds, or until the chocolate is melted and the mixture is frothy. Taste for sweetness; add sugar if necessary, and blend for a few more seconds.

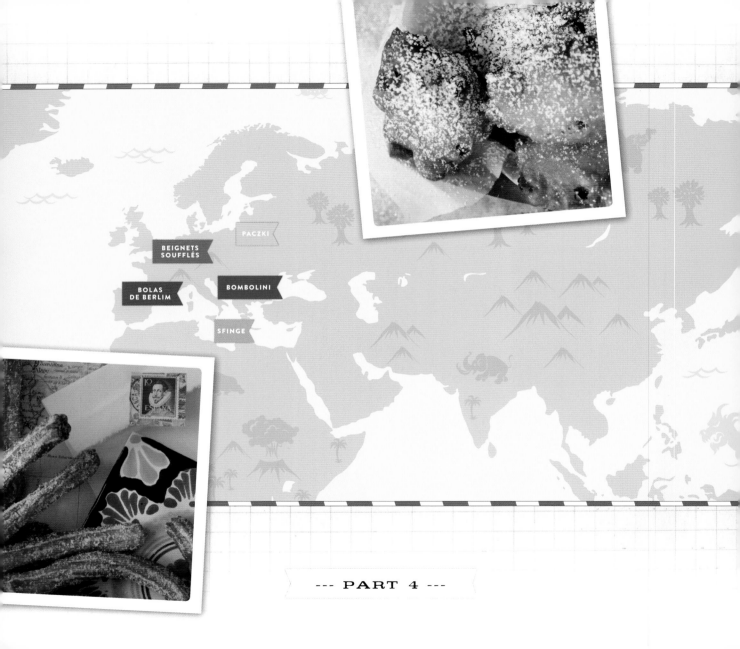

BEIGNETS
SOUFFLÉS

PACZKI

BOLAS
DE BERLIM

BOMBOLINI

SFINGE

--- PART 4 ---

EUROPE

While many American doughnut styles can be traced back to European culinary traditions, the ring-shaped American doughnut has never been the European style. (And somehow, Europeans have never quite adopted the American fondness for rainbow-colored sprinkles and crayon-bright icings, either.) Instead, the sweet fried doughs and batters of France, Spain, Portugal, Italy, Germany, and Holland come in free-form rounds or plump spheres, star-shaped tubes, or as golden coatings over clusters of dried fruit.

The history of European doughnuts is one of festivity and celebration. Frying called for lavish amounts of fat, usually lard, and sugar was an expensive indulgence beyond the everyday means of most ordinary cooks, as were aromatic, flavorings brought back along the Spice Road, including sweet vanilla, fragrant nutmeg, mace, and tongue-tingling ginger. (Cinnamon, however, so ubiquitous in American sweets, is a rarity in European pastry.)

Sweet, fragrantly spiced fried pastries were saved for special occasions, usually connected with church holidays. Carnival, the pre-Lenten season of indulgence and riotous living before weeks of austerity, was heralded with numerous types of sugary fried cakes, from the Venetian frittelle, or fritters, made with raisins and pine nuts, to the rich Polish paczki, filled with sweet cherry or plum jam. Fasching, the German Carnival, was celebrated with sugar-rolled, jelly-filled doughnuts called pfannkuchen, berliners, or faschnachts, the model for the typical American jelly doughnut. (Faschnachts could also be made without fillings, the dough shaped into rings, knots, braids, or pretzels, sometimes dipped into sugar syrup after frying.) With a traditional church calendar that called for many weeks and days of fasting or spare, meatless meals, gastronomic indulgence was enjoyed in all its all-too-brief glory on saints' days and festivals, whose seasonal timing often overlapped with much older pagan celebrations.

Fairs and local festivals were also a source of sweet treats, since fairgoers came with money in their pockets, ready for amusement and delight. It didn't take much to set up as an itinerant doughnut-maker on a market day or during a festival, and the investment usually paid back many times over, as few could resist the sugary siren call of a hot fried dumpling, fruit fritter, or sweet fried pie, cheap at the price.

In Northern and Central European countries, with their shorter growing seasons and longer winters, preserved fruits and jams were used more often in desserts than fresh fruit, and so a tradition of jam- and jelly-filled dumplings and dough puffs evolved. Walnuts, hazelnuts, almonds, poppy seeds, almond paste, and dried fruits were part of the pastry cook's larder, too.

Down along the Adriatic and the Mediterranean, warmer climates and centuries of Arabic and Moorish influence meant pastries flavored with citrus and spices, some dipped in honey syrups, perfumed with orange-flower water, or filled with creamy fresh cheese. In Portugal, convent communities of nuns became famous for producing dense, golden custards and sweets rich with egg yolks. This eggy legacy persists in a German import, bolas de Berlim, yeast-raised puffs of dough with an egg-rich, Portuguese-style pastry cream bursting through a slit in the side. In Spain, rich, thick hot chocolate has been part of the culinary heritage since the original conquistadors brought the cacao bean back from Mexico. After a night of eating, drinking, and entertainment, nothing is as restorative as a cup of hot chocolate. But you can't have chocolate without a churro to dunk in it, made with a buttery, choux-pastry batter just like the one used in France for éclairs and profiteroles. A bite, a thick, warming sip, another sugar-crunched bite, and the day can begin. Who needs sleep?

BEIGNETS SOUFFLÉS

MAKES 24 BEIGNETS SOUFFLÉS

In France, the term BEIGNET *usually refers to a small, savory fritter. Beignets soufflés, how-ever, are sweet, delectable puffs, made from the same buttery, eggy batter used for profiteroles and éclairs. Dropped into hot oil, they swell and expand into a rich treat that needs only a dust-ing of powdered sugar. A batch of these will transport you to your favorite Parisian café or salon de thé. Serve with a pot of Earl Grey tea, whose bergamot perfume echoes their delicate orange blossom scent. Look for orange-flower water in specialty groceries or Middle Eastern markets.*

1 cup water

6 tablespoons unsalted butter

1 tablespoon granulated sugar

½ teaspoon salt

1 cup unbleached all-purpose flour

4 large eggs

1 tablespoon brandy

1 tablespoon orange-flower water

Vegetable oil for deep-frying

Powdered sugar for dusting

1. In a medium saucepan, combine the water, butter, the sugar, and the salt. Bring to a boil over medium-high heat, then reduce the heat to low. Using a wooden spoon, stir in the flour and cook, stirring constantly, until the mixture pulls away from the sides of the pan and forms a ball.

2. Remove from the heat and let cool for 1 minute. Vigor-ously beat in the eggs, one at a time, making sure each egg is thoroughly absorbed before adding the next. At first, the mixture will be slippery and resistant, but persist; each egg will be easier to beat in than the one before it. Beat in the brandy and orange-flower water. Set aside.

PG. 115

CONTINUED ------------------>

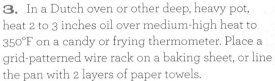

3. In a Dutch oven or other deep, heavy pot, heat 2 to 3 inches oil over medium-high heat to 350°F on a candy or frying thermometer. Place a grid-patterned wire rack on a baking sheet, or line the pan with 2 layers of paper towels.

4. Dip 2 teaspoons briefly into the hot oil. Scoop up a spoonful of batter in one spoon, then push it off into the hot oil with the other spoon. Fry for about 30 seconds, then turn over with a slotted spoon or a skimmer and fry for another 30 seconds, or until puffed, pale golden brown and cooked through but still moist inside.

5. Using a slotted spoon or a skimmer, transfer the fried dough to the wire rack or paper towels to drain and cool slightly. Repeat to cook the remaining batter. Dust the warm rounds with powdered sugar. Transfer to a platter and serve warm.

CHURROS
AND SPANISH-STYLE HOT CHOCOLATE

MAKES 10 TO 12 CHURROS

In Spain, hot chocolate is just that: a lavish amount of dark chocolate melted into milk to make a rich, almost pudding-thick drink. And just as Americans dunk their doughnuts in coffee, no Spaniard feels a cup of CHOCOLADA CALDA *is complete without a sugar-coated churro for dipping. Professional churro-makers squeeze their batter through a special ridged tube into the hot oil in order to give more crunchy fried surface area to the finished product. You can get the same effect by using a pastry bag with a large star tip.*

1 cup water

6 tablespoons unsalted butter

1 tablespoon sugar, plus more for coating

¼ teaspoon salt

1 cup unbleached all-purpose flour

3 large eggs

Vegetable oil for deep-frying

Spanish-Style Hot Chocolate for serving (recipe follows)

1. In a medium saucepan, combine the water, butter, the 1 tablespoon sugar, and the salt. Bring to a boil over medium-high heat, then reduce the heat to low. Using a wooden spoon, stir in the flour and cook, stirring constantly, until the mixture pulls away from the sides of the pan and forms a ball.

2. Remove from the heat and let cool for 1 minute. Vigorously beat in the eggs, one at a time, making sure each egg is thoroughly absorbed before adding the next. At first, the mixture will be slippery and resistant, but persist; each egg will be easier to beat in than the one before it. Set aside.

PG. 117

CONTINUED ------→

3. In a Dutch oven or other deep, heavy pot, heat 2 to 3 inches oil over medium-high heat to 350°F on a candy or frying thermometer. Place a grid-patterned wire rack on a baking sheet, or line the pan with two layers of paper towels. Pour sugar for coating the churros into a wide, shallow bowl.

4. Spoon the batter into a pastry bag fitted with a large star tip. Squeeze tubes of dough 5 to 6 inches long into the hot oil in batches, being careful not to crowd the pan. Fry, turning with tongs, until golden brown and cooked through but still moist inside, 5 to 8 minutes.

5. Using tongs, transfer the churros to the wire rack or paper towels to drain and cool slightly. As soon as the churros are cool enough to handle, roll them in the sugar. Serve warm, with the hot chocolate.

SPANISH-STYLE HOT CHOCOLATE

SERVES 6

1 tablespoon cornstarch

4 cups whole milk

8 ounces semisweet or bittersweet chocolate, chopped

1. In a small bowl, add the cornstarch to ¼ cup of the milk and stir until dissolved. In a medium saucepan, combine the remaining 3¾ cups milk, the cornstarch mixture, and chocolate and bring to a simmer over medium heat, whisking frequently, until the chocolate is melted.

2. Reduce the heat to medium-low and simmer gently, whisking frequently, for 3 minutes. Remove from the heat and let stand for a few minutes. (The mixture will continue to thicken as it stands.)

3. Pour into small cups and serve with churros for dipping.

BOLAS DE BERLIM

MAKES 12 TO 14 BOLAS DE BERLIM

A version of these Portuguese sweets, called sonhos ("dreams") is popular in Brazil. Instead of piping in the eggy custard filling, bolas are slashed open and the cream spooned in so it's fully visible (and appetite-whetting).

1½ teaspoons active dry yeast

2 tablespoons warm water

½ cup milk

¼ cup sugar

2 tablespoons unsalted butter

½ teaspoon salt

2 cups unbleached all-purpose flour

1 large egg

Vegetable oil for deep-frying

Creme de Pasteleiro (recipe follows)

Powdered sugar for dusting

1. In a small bowl, sprinkle the yeast over the warm water. Let stand for 5 minutes, then stir to dissolve the yeast.

2. In a medium saucepan, heat the milk over medium-low heat until bubbles form around the edges of the pan. Remove from the heat and add the sugar, butter, and salt, stirring until the butter is melted.

3. Add the flour to the bowl of a stand mixer fitted with the dough hook. Make a well in the center of the flour. Add the milk mixture to the well and start mixing on low speed. Add the yeast mixture and continue mixing. Add the egg and increase the speed to medium. Continue mixing until the dough is smooth and elastic, 3 to 4 minutes. If necessary, scrape down the sides of the bowl with a rubber spatula.

4. Transfer the dough to a lightly oiled bowl and turn to coat. Cover with a damp clean kitchen towel and let rise in a warm place for 1 hour, or until doubled in bulk.

5. Lightly flour a work surface and a baking sheet. Gently punch down the dough. On the floured work surface, form the dough into a ball and divide it into 12 to 14 pieces. Roll into balls about the size of a golf ball. Arrange on the floured pan, cover with a clean dry kitchen towel, and let rise again for 25 to 30 minutes, or until light and puffy.

6. In a Dutch oven or other deep, heavy pot, heat 2 to 3 inches oil over medium-high heat to 365°F on a candy or frying thermometer. Place a grid-patterned wire rack on a baking sheet, or line the pan with two layers of paper towels.

7. Using a slotted spoon or a skimmer, drop the balls into the hot oil in batches, being careful not to crowd the pan. Fry for about 1 minute per side, or until the doughnuts are puffed, golden brown, and cooked through. Using a slotted spoon or a skimmer, transfer to the wire rack or paper towels to drain. Let cool to room temperature.

8. Slit a doughnut open along one side, cutting halfway through the doughnut. Spoon in about a tablespoon of the chilled pastry cream. Arrange the doughnuts on a serving plate and dust them with the powdered sugar. Serve now, or refrigerate for up to 3 hours.

CONTINUED ⟶

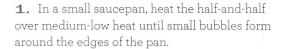

CREME DE PASTELEIRO

MAKES 1¼ CUPS

1 cup half-and-half

4 large egg yolks

⅓ cup sugar

1½ tablespoons cornstarch

1 teaspoon vanilla extract

1. In a small saucepan, heat the half-and-half over medium-low heat until small bubbles form around the edges of the pan.

2. In a medium bowl, using a whisk or a hand-held electric mixer, beat the egg yolks briefly. Sift the sugar and cornstarch together. Beat the sugar mixture into the egg yolks until the mixture is smooth and thick. In a slow but steady stream, gradually but vigorously whisk in the hot milk.

3. Transfer the mixture to a heavy medium saucepan. Over medium heat, whisk vigorously until the mixture begins to thicken. Reduce the heat to low and whisk until the mixture is thick and glossy. Remove from the heat.

4. Beat the vanilla extract into the pastry cream. Scoop into a bowl and press plastic wrap directly onto the surface of the pastry cream to prevent a skin from forming. Cover and refrigerate until thoroughly chilled, at least 2 hours or up to 3 days.

BOMBOLINI

MAKES 12 BOMBOLINI

These puffy yeast-raised Italian doughnuts are typically filled with jelly or rich custard, then dusted with sugar. But some gelato shops use unfilled bombolini to make deliciously decadent gelato "panini," splitting the pastry along the side like a roll, then stuffing them with scoops of gelato.

1½ teaspoons active dry yeast

2 tablespoons warm water

2 cups bread flour

3 tablespoons granulated sugar

½ teaspoon salt

2 large eggs

Grated zest of ½ lemon

⅓ cup water

4 tablespoons unsalted butter, softened

Vegetable oil for deep-frying

1 cup jelly

Powdered sugar for dusting

1. In a small bowl, sprinkle the yeast over the water. Let stand for 5 minutes, then stir to dissolve the yeast.

2. Add the flour, the granulated sugar, and the salt together into the bowl of a stand mixer fitted with the dough hook. Add the eggs, yeast mixture, lemon zest, and water and mix to a soft dough. Add the butter, 1 tablespoon at a time, and continue mixing for 6 to 8 minutes, or until the dough is ropy and stretchy.

3. Lightly oil a deep bowl. Place the dough in the bowl and turn it to coat with oil. Cover and let rise in the refrigerator until doubled in bulk, 6 to 8 hours or overnight.

CONTINUED ------->

4. Punch down the dough. Lightly flour a work surface and 2 baking sheets. On the floured work surface, form the dough into a ball, then divide into 12 pieces and roll into balls. Arrange the balls on the floured baking sheets. Cover loosely with plastic wrap and let rise in a warm place for about 1½ hours, or until doubled in size.

5. In a Dutch oven or other deep, heavy pot, heat 2 to 3 inches oil over medium-high heat to 375°F on a candy or frying thermometer. Place a grid-patterned wire rack on a baking sheet, or line the pan with two layers of paper towels.

6. Using a slotted spoon or a skimmer, drop the doughnuts into hot oil in the batches, being careful not to crowd the pan. Fry for 1 to 2 minutes per side, or until puffed, golden brown, and cooked through.

7. Using a slotted spoon or a skimmer, transfer the doughnuts to the wire rack or paper towels to drain.

8. Spoon the jelly into a pastry bag fitted with a plain tip. Using the end of a chopstick or the tip of a knife, poke a small hole in the top of the doughnut. Insert the tip of the pastry bag and squeeze in a generous teaspoonful of jelly. Dust with powdered sugar on both sides. Transfer to a platter and serve warm or at room temperature.

ZEPPOLE

MAKES 12 ZEPPOLE

Zeppole di San Giuseppe have long been served on March 19 in Italy for the Feast of St. Joseph, patron saint of pastry chefs. Some tradition-minded Italian bakeries still make them only once a year, while others, knowing their customers will buy a good thing when they taste it no matter what the season, fry them up for several weeks between St. Joseph's Day and Easter. This version, filled with pastry cream and cherries, is typically Neapolitan. True Italian zeppole bear little resemblance to the funnel-cake-like squiggles of plain, sugar-dusted fried dough sold under the same name at many American street fairs and carnivals.

1⅓ cups water

6 tablespoons unsalted butter, cut into chunks

1 tablespoon granulated sugar

½ teaspoon salt

1⅓ cups unbleached all-purpose flour

5 large eggs

Vegetable oil for deep-frying

Vanilla Custard Filling (page 59)

Powdered sugar for dusting

½ cup amarena cherries, drained (optional); see notes, page 127

1. In a medium saucepan, combine the water, butter, sugar, and salt. Bring to a boil over medium-high heat. Reduce the heat to low. Using a wooden spoon, stir in the flour and cook, stirring constantly, until the mixture pulls away from the sides of the pan and forms a ball, about 4 minutes.

CONTINUED ⟶

2. Remove from the heat and let cool for a few minutes. Beat in the eggs, one at a time, beating vigorously and making sure each egg is thoroughly absorbed before adding the next. At first, the mixture will be slippery and resistant, but persist; each egg will be easier to beat in than the one before it. Beat until the dough is smooth.

3. In a Dutch oven or other deep, heavy pot, heat 2 to 3 inches oil over medium-high heat to 360°F on a candy or frying thermometer. Place a grid-patterned wire rack on a baking sheet, or line the pan with two layers of paper towels.

4. While the oil is heating, spoon the batter into a pastry bag fitted with a ½-inch star tip. Cut parchment paper into twelve 4-inch squares. Pipe a ring of batter onto each square.

5. Using a slotted spoon or a skimmer, slide 3 to 4 parchment squares into the hot oil, being careful not to crowd the pan. Fry for 3 to 4 minutes on each side, or until puffed, golden brown, and cooked through, turning as necessary.

6. Using a slotted spoon or a skimmer, transfer the zeppole to the wire rack or paper towels to drain. Repeat with the remaining dough. Let the doughnuts cool to room temperature.

7. Spoon the chilled custard filling into a pastry bag fitted with a ½-inch star tip. Pipe a small round of custard atop each zeppole. Dust with powdered sugar. If desired, add a cherry in the center.

NOTES: You can also drop spoonfuls of batter directly onto the hot oil to make simple fried puffs. Serve with warm Chocolate Rum Sauce (page 67) on the side for dunking.

Amarena cherries are small, dark, tart cherries grown in the Emilio-Romagna region of central Italy. They are pitted and soaked in a sugar syrup. You can find them in Italian groceries and specialty markets.

Variation:

LEMON- OR ORANGE-FILLED ZEPPOLE

Substitute the grated zest of 1 lemon or orange for the vanilla bean in the Custard Filling recipe, letting it steep as directed and then straining it out before proceeding with the remainder of the recipe.

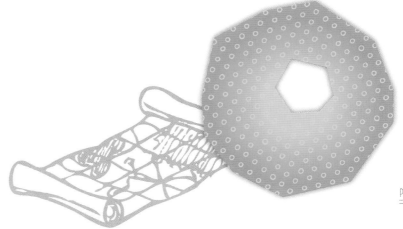

SICILY

SFINGE

MAKES 12 SFINGE

Sfinge, like zeppole, are made from an eggy choux-pastry dough and served in honor of St. Joseph on March 19, now also celebrated as Father's Day in Italy. But where the Neapolitan zeppole are filled with pastry cream, the Sicilian sfinge are stuffed with sweetened ricotta, much like cannoli, and topped with a sprinkling of pistachio nuts. You can also add a couple tablespoons of chopped dark chocolate to the filling.

Zeppole (page 125)

2 tablespoons pistachio nuts, coarsely chopped

FILLING

1¼ pounds whole-milk ricotta (look for fresh ricotta sold in bulk in Italian groceries, specialty markets, or cheese shops)

½ cup sugar

1 teaspoon vanilla extract

⅓ cup candied orange peel, finely chopped

1. Prepare the zeppole but do not add the custard filling.

2. FOR THE FILLING: Using the back of a large spoon, push the ricotta through a fine-meshed sieve into a large bowl. Using a hand-held electric mixer, beat in the sugar and vanilla and continue beating until the mixture is very smooth. Stir in the orange peel.

3. Spoon the ricotta filling into a pastry bag fitted with a ½-inch star tip. Pipe the filling in a 2-inch round atop each zeppole and sprinkle with pistachios. Or, split the zeppole open and pipe a round of filling inside. Pipe a very small round of filling on top of the pastry and sprinkle with pistachios.

BACI

MAKES 25 TO 28 FRITTERS

Having a Valentine's Day party? These plump little Italian BACI, *or kisses, make an especially alluring dessert for a small crowd. Taste one, and before you know it, you'll be popping another right into the mouth of that swell-looking honey next to you. If you have a good Italian deli or cheese store in your area, look for fresh, locally made ricotta. If you get really lucky, you might even find fresh sheep's milk ricotta, whose delicate, milky richness will turn these into* BACI DEGLI ANGELI—*angels' kisses.*

1 cup (8 ounces) whole-milk ricotta cheese

2 large eggs

½ cup unbleached all-purpose flour

1 tablespoon granulated sugar

1½ teaspoons baking powder

¼ teaspoon ground cinnamon

⅛ teaspoon salt

1 teaspoon grated orange zest

½ teaspoon vanilla extract

Vegetable oil for deep-frying

Powdered sugar for dusting

1. In a medium bowl and using a hand-held electric mixer, beat the ricotta and eggs on medium speed until smooth. Sift the flour, sugar, baking powder, cinnamon, and salt together into the ricotta mixture. Mix on low speed until smooth. Stir in the orange zest and vanilla.

2. In a Dutch oven or other deep, heavy pot, heat 2 to 3 inches oil over medium-high heat to 365°F on a candy or frying thermometer. Place a grid-patterned wire rack on a baking sheet, or line the pan with two layers of paper towels.

PG. 129

CONTINUED ·······························→

3. Scoop up teaspoonfuls of the ricotta mixture and drop into the hot oil in batches, being careful not to crowd the pan. Cook for about 1 minute on each side, or until golden brown and cooked through but still moist inside. Repeat with the remaining batter.

4. Using a slotted spoon or a skimmer, transfer to the wire rack or paper towels to drain. Let cool slightly, then transfer to a serving plate and dust with powdered sugar. Pile the fritters in a pyramid, dust with a little more powdered sugar, and serve warm.

NOTE: These fritters are best served warm and fresh from the fryer. If necessary, fry half the batch, dust with powdered sugar, and serve. Continue frying the remaining batter once the first batch has been devoured.

FRITTELLE

MAKES 12 TO 14 FRITTELLE

Studded with raisins and pine nuts, these small, golden fritters are a traditional food for Carnival in Venice, dating back at least to the Renaissance. Now, they're flavored many different ways, some with chopped apples instead of raisins, others filled with pastry cream.

2 tablespoons grappa

2 tablespoons raisins

1 package (2¼ teaspoons) active dry yeast

¼ cup warm water (110° to 115°F)

1¾ cups unbleached all-purpose flour

¼ cup granulated sugar

½ teaspoon salt

1 cup milk, warmed

1 large egg yolk

2 tablespoons pine nuts

¼ teaspoon aniseeds (optional)

Vegetable oil for deep-frying

Powdered sugar for dusting

1. In a small bowl, pour the grappa over the raisins and set aside. In another small bowl, sprinkle the yeast over the warm water. Let stand for 5 minutes, then stir to dissolve the yeast.

2. Add the flour, granulated sugar, and salt to a stand mixer fitted with the dough hook. Make a well in the center and add the milk, egg yolk, and yeast mixture. Beat on medium speed for 4 to 6 minutes, or until a smooth, spongy batter is formed. Beat in the raisins (and any remaining grappa), pine nuts, and aniseeds, if using.

CONTINUED -------------→

3. Cover with a damp clean kitchen towel or plastic wrap. Let rise in a warm place for 1 to 1½ hours, or until bubbly and doubled in size.

4. In a Dutch oven or other deep, heavy pot, heat 2 to 3 inches oil over medium-high heat to 365°F on a candy or frying thermometer. Place a grid-patterned wire rack on a baking sheet, or line the pan with two layers of paper towels.

5. Gently stir down the batter. Dip 2 teaspoons briefly into the hot oil. Scoop up a spoonful of batter in one spoon, making sure to include some raisins and pine nuts, then push it off into the hot oil with the other spoon. Fry for about 30 seconds, then turn over with a slotted spoon or a skimmer and fry for another 30 seconds, or until puffed, pale golden brown, and cooked through but still moist inside. Using a slotted spoon or a skimmer, transfer the frittelle to the wire rack or paper towels to drain.

6. Let cool slightly. Arrange on a platter. Dust with powdered sugar and serve warm.

PACZKI

MAKES 9 TO 10 PACZKI

Pronounced "POOCH-KEY," these doughnuts are richer but less sweet than a typical jelly doughnut. They're a crucial part of Polish (and Polish-American) pre-Lenten festivities. Old recipes could call for up to a dozen eggs, beaten until thick and fluffy, sometimes mixed with boiled mashed potatoes, other times with cream.

Note: This recipe uses a starter, a thin batter of yeast, milk, and flour.

1 package (2¼ teaspoons) active dry yeast

1 cup warm milk (110° to 115°F)

2½ cups unbleached all-purpose flour

3 large egg yolks

¼ cup granulated sugar

½ teaspoon salt

2 tablespoons unsalted butter, melted

Vegetable oil for deep-frying

1 cup fruit preserves, such as cherry, plum, or rose hip

Powdered sugar for dusting

1. FOR THE STARTER: In a medium bowl, sprinkle the yeast over the warm milk. Let stand for 5 minutes, then stir to dissolve the yeast. Using a wooden spoon, gradually beat in 1 cup of the flour to make a thick batter. Cover with a damp clean kitchen towel and let stand in a warm place for 30 to 40 minutes, or until bubbly.

2. In a large bowl, using a hand-held electric mixer on medium speed, beat the egg yolks and granulated sugar until the mixture is thick and pale, about 4 minutes.

PG. 133

CONTINUED ------------→

3. Stir the salt and melted butter into the starter, then add the starter to the egg mixture, beating until smooth. Gradually beat in 1 cup of the flour and beat on medium speed until the dough becomes too thick to mix. Using a wooden spoon, beat in the remaining ½ cup of flour by hand to form a soft, sticky dough.

4. Transfer the dough to a lightly oiled bowl. Turn the dough to coat it with oil. Cover with a damp clean kitchen towel or plastic wrap and let rise in a warm place for 1 hour, or until doubled in size.

5. Lightly flour a work surface and a baking sheet. Gently punch down the dough and turn it out onto the floured work surface. Using a well-floured rolling pin, roll the dough into a ½-inch-thick round. Using a floured 3-inch biscuit cutter, cut out rounds, flouring the cutter between each cut, and transfer the rounds to the floured baking sheet. Cover with a dry clean kitchen towel and let rise again in a warm place for 30 minutes, or until light, puffy, and nearly doubled in size.

6. In a Dutch oven or other deep, heavy pot, heat 2 to 3 inches oil over medium-high heat to 365°F on a candy or frying thermometer. Place a grid-patterned wire rack on a baking sheet, or line the pan with two layers of paper towels.

7. Using a slotted spoon or a skimmer, drop the paczki into the hot oil in batches, making sure not to crowd the pan. Fry for 1 to 2 minutes on each side, or until golden brown and cooked through. Using a slotted spoon or a skimmer, transfer to the wire rack or paper towels to drain. Let cool to room temperature.

8. Spoon the preserves into a pastry bag fitted with a plain ¼-inch tip. Using the end of a chop-stick or the tip of a small, sharp knife, make a hole in the side of each round. Insert the pastry tip and squeeze a generous teaspoon of preserves into each doughnut.

9. Dust both sides of the filled doughnuts with powdered sugar.

OLIEBOLLEN

MAKES 12 TO 14 OLIEBOLLEN

Who needs Champagne when you've got oliebollen? For centuries, these Dutch treats have been served throughout the winter holidays, but especially on New Year's Eve. Special stands and food trucks specializing in oliebollen start appearing in Dutch cities by mid-November, and everyone has an opinion about which ones are best. In fact, the Dutch newspaper AD runs a country-wide "oliebollentest" that's published during the last week of the year, with no-holds-barred comments on the one hundred best (and worst) oliebollen in the country.

½ cup raisins or currants, or a mixture of the two

1 cup milk

¼ cup lager-type beer

1 package (2¼ teaspoons) active dry yeast

1⅔ cups unbleached all-purpose flour

½ teaspoon salt

1 tablespoon granulated sugar

1 large egg

1 tablespoon unsalted butter, softened

1 tart apple, such as Granny Smith, peeled, cored, and finely chopped, mixed with 1 teaspoon lemon juice to prevent browning (optional)

Vegetable oil for deep-frying

Powdered sugar for dusting

1. Put the raisins in a small bowl and add hot water to cover. Set aside.

2. In a small saucepan, combine the milk and beer. Heat over medium-low heat to 110° to 115°F. Pour the milk mixture into a small bowl and sprinkle the yeast over it. Let stand for 5 minutes, then stir to dissolve the yeast.

3. Add the flour, salt, and granulated sugar to the bowl of a stand mixer fitted with a dough hook. Make a well in the center and pour in the

CONTINUED ------->

yeast mixture. Mix on medium speed until the mixture comes together and the flour is absorbed.

4. Beat in the egg and butter and continue mixing until a soft, smooth dough is formed. Drain the raisins well, patting off any excess water with a towel. Mix in the raisins and chopped apple, if using.

5. Transfer the dough to a lightly oiled bowl and turn the dough to coat it with oil. Cover with a damp clean kitchen towel or plastic wrap and let rise in a warm place for 1 hour, or until doubled in size.

6. In a Dutch oven or other deep, heavy pot, heat 2 to 3 inches oil over medium-high heat to 365°F on a candy or frying thermometer. Place a grid-patterned wire rack on a baking sheet, or line the pan with two layers of paper towels.

7. Dip two tablespoons briefly into the hot oil. Scoop as much dough as you can hold in one spoon. Hold the spoon over the surface of the oil and push the dough into the oil with the second spoon. Repeat 5 or 6 times, taking care not to crowd the pan. Fry for 1 to 2 minutes per side, turning as necessary, until golden brown and cooked through.

8. Using a slotted spoon or a skimmer, transfer the oliebollen to the wire rack or paper towels to drain. Repeat with the remaining dough.

9. Arrange on a serving platter and dust with powdered sugar. Serve warm.

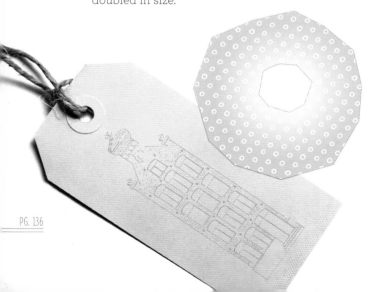

PFANNKUCHEN

MAKES 12 PFANNKUCHEN

The great-grandma of the jelly doughnut is now a staple at every American doughnut shop. They came over with the waves of nineteenth-century German immigrants who settled throughout the United States, especially in the Midwest. They have also become a specialty of the Pennsylvania Dutch communities, "Dutch" being a corruption of DEUTSCH, meaning German.

1 package (2¼ teaspoons) active dry yeast

2 tablespoons warm water

2 cups unbleached all-purpose flour

3 tablespoons granulated sugar

¼ teaspoon salt

½ cup warm milk (110° to 115°F)

2 large eggs, separated

2 tablespoons unsalted butter, cut into bits and softened

1 cup jelly

Vegetable oil for deep-frying

Powdered sugar for dusting

1. In a small bowl, sprinkle the yeast over the warm water. Let stand for 5 minutes, then stir to dissolve the yeast.

2. Add the flour, granulated sugar, and salt to the bowl of a stand mixer fitted with the dough hook. Stir the flour mixture with a whisk to blend. Make a well in the center. Pour in the yeast mixture and warm milk. Mix on low speed until the mixture begins to form a soft dough. Beat in the egg yolks, one at a time.

When the egg yolks are absorbed, add the butter and mix on medium speed until the dough is smooth and elastic, 3 to 4 minutes.

3. Transfer to a lightly oiled bowl and turn the dough to coat it with oil. Cover with a damp clean kitchen towel or plastic wrap and let rise in a warm place for 1 hour, or until doubled in size.

4. Lightly flour a work surface and a baking sheet. Turn the dough out onto the floured work surface. Using a rolling pin, roll the dough out in a ½-inch-thick round. Using a floured 3-inch biscuit cutter, cut the dough into rounds, flouring the cutter between each cut to prevent sticking. Transfer half the rounds to the floured baking sheet.

5. Place ½ teaspoon of jelly in the center of each round. Using a pastry brush, brush the edges of the filled rounds with egg white. Place a second circle of dough on top and press firmly to seal the edges. Cover with a dry clean kitchen towel and let rise in a warm place for 20 minutes, or until light and puffy.

6. In a Dutch oven or other deep, heavy pot, heat 2 to 3 inches oil over medium-high heat to 365°F on a candy or frying thermometer. Place a grid-patterned wire rack on a baking sheet, or line the pan with two layers of paper towels.

7. Using a slotted spoon or a skimmer, lower the doughnuts into the hot oil in batches, being careful not to crowd the pan. Fry for 2 to 3 minutes on each side until golden brown and cooked through.

8. Using a slotted spoon or a skimmer, transfer the doughnuts to the wire rack or paper towels to drain.

9. Dust both sides of the doughnuts with powdered sugar. Arrange on a platter and serve warm or at room temperature.

SFENJ

LOUKOUMADES

AWWAMAT

GULAB JAMUN

BÁNH CAM

--- PART 5 ---

THE EASTERN AND SOUTHERN MEDITERRANEAN AND ASIA

From Morocco, Algeria, and Tunisia in the southwest to Greece and Turkey in the northeast, and Egypt, Israel, Lebanon, and Syria in the southeast, the cultures and countries of the eastern and southern Mediterranean share a complicated, crisscrossing history. After the collapse of the Roman Empire, centuries of Arabic and Persian conquest and rule from the Middle East shaped every aspect of life, from food and medicine to poetry and religion.

Throughout the Mediterranean and the Middle East, drifts of starry white blossoms float on the breeze as the almond trees come into bloom in the springtime. Come fall, wide-spreading fig trees drop heavy soft-skinned fruits, some dusty indigo, others yellow green, some candy-striped pink. Pomegranate branches are tipped with heavy garnet balls, rough skins cracked open to reveal the ruby jewels within. By the cool, wet weather of January, lemons, citrons, blood oranges, and tangerines glow as brightly as Christmas ornaments between pointed dark green leaves. Pistachios, saffron, roses, dates, cardamom, quinces, orange blossoms—all offer their flavors, scents, and nuances to Mediterranean and Middle Eastern tables.

Even now, centuries later, the Arabic influence on the entire region can still be tasted. In Greece and Turkey, as in Lebanon and Syria, the sweet tooth is very sweet, and more often than not, fried pastries are served glistening like amber under a glossy cloak of honey or sugar syrup. In Greece, loukoumades make a frequent appearance, alongside strong, sweet ink-black coffee; in Turkey, the doughnuts of choice may be perfumed with cardamom and drizzled with rosewater syrup. In the Sephardic Jewish cultures of North Africa, mint tea and coffee are paired with sfenj, rings of light, eggy yeast dough fragrant with orange zest. These doughnuts, among many other fried sweet treats and fritters, are especially popular during both the Carnival-like Purim holiday and Hanukkah, the Jewish festival of lights that's celebrated in part by eating foods fried in oil.

During the eight days of Hanukkah, Israelis offer plates of sufganiyot, powdered-sugar doughnuts filled with jelly, to friends and family. They may be Israeli now, but their roots lie in the gastronomic heritage of the many German and Central European immigrants who settled there. Israel's favorite foods may be the falafel, hummus, and pita of the Mideast, but its sufganiyot are Germany's pfannkuchen, transplanted.

Heading further east, to China, Vietnam, and India, the fried sweets (and savories) shift again. In China, the sweet tooth of the Middle East disappears, replaced by cravings for things salty and savory. A simple, comforting rice porridge called congee or jook can be flavored dozens of ways, but it makes a popular breakfast at home or in a café or street-side stall. Long, unsweetened sticks of golden fried dough, known as you tiao, or crullers, are always served alongside for dunking and munching; they're also enjoyed with a glass of sweet or salty warm soy milk. You tiao (literally, "oil ghosts") are rarely made at home; instead, they're eaten fresh from street vendors, or bought frozen and reheated to crispness in the home oven. Similar crullers, under different names, can be found from Laos, Myanmar, and Thailand to Indonesia and the Philippines. In Vietnam, the same crullers might accompany a variety of soups and herb-strewn noodle broths, while bánh cam, sesame balls filled with sweetened mung beans, make a pleasant light snack with a fragrant pot of jasmine tea.

In the heat of India, a fondness for sweets returns with a vengeance, balanced by the irresistible bounty of salty, oily snacks. Street stalls and tea shops sell dozens of different types of sweets, many made from creamy caramelized milk and sugar boiled down into fudge, others from brightly colored dough twirled into fanciful swirls and spirals in vats of bubbling ghee, then soaked in fragrant sugar syrups. Such treats are particularly popular during Diwali, the Hindu festival of lights, when every village is festooned with lights and hanging lanterns, and gifts of sweets are traditionally shared between family and friends.

Two of the most popular fried sweets are gulab jamun, small, puffy milk-based dough balls soaked in sugar syrup, and jalebis, skinny coils of light, crisp dough, often dyed yellow, orange, or red and glazed with syrup. In An Invitation to Indian Cooking, author Madhur Jaffrey describes the tea breaks punctuating every Indian workday. Friends and coworkers would gather at a nearby snack shop, where the "very spicy hot samosas and the sugary-sweet gulab jamun were eaten simultaneously—a bite of one balancing a bite of the other and each swallowed with a soothing sip of scalding hot tea." In the famed tea province of Assam, between Burma and Tibet, rice-flour fritters called pithas are a local favorite, especially the ones known as koat pithas, flavored with jaggery (coarse, unrefined palm or cane sugar, similar to Mexican piloncillo) and mashed banana. In taste, they could be a cousin to bonelos agas, the fried banana balls found among the Pacific Islands in Guam and the Philippines, where fried sweets often rely on local produce like bananas, squashes, and tropical tubers.

LOUKOUMADES

MAKES 15 TO 18 LOUKOUMADES

In Greece, the midnight church bells tolling for Easter Sunday also mark the arrival of these much-loved doughnuts, glossed with honey and scattered with crushed walnuts and a sprinkle of cinnamon. Of course, they're also eaten at other times of the year, but their delightful honey-dripping sweetness is particularly appreciated after the austerity of Lent.

Pure olive oil is traditional for frying these doughnuts; because olive oil has a lower smoke point than other vegetable oils, loukoumades should be fried at a lower temperature than usual.

1 package (2¼ teaspoons) active dry yeast

2 to 2¼ cups warm water (110° to 115°F)

2 cups unbleached all-purpose flour

1 teaspoon salt

1 teaspoon grated lemon zest (optional)

Pure olive oil or vegetable oil for deep-frying

½ cup honey, warmed

½ cup chopped walnuts, almonds, or pistachios

Ground cinnamon for dusting

1. In a small bowl, sprinkle the yeast over 1 cup of the warm water. Let stand for 5 minutes, then stir to dissolve the yeast.

2. Add the flour and salt to the bowl of a stand mixer fitted with a dough hook; stir to blend. Make a well in the center and pour in the yeast mixture and lemon zest, if using. Beat on low speed, adding additional water as necessary to make a very loose, ropy dough; it should be too loose to knead by hand. Knead for an additional minute or two.

3. Scrape the dough into a clean bowl and cover with a damp clean kitchen towel or plastic wrap. Let stand in a warm place for 1 hour, or until bubbly.

CONTINUED ⟶

4. In a Dutch oven or other deep, heavy pot, heat 2 to 3 inches oil over medium-high heat to 325°F on a candy or frying thermometer. Place a grid-patterned rack on a baking sheet, or line the pan with two layers of paper towels.

5. Dip 2 tablespoons into the hot oil. Scoop up a tablespoonful of batter in one spoon, then use the other spoon to push the batter off the spoon into the hot oil. Repeat with remaining batter, working in batches and being careful not to crowd the pan.

6. Fry the loukoumades for 2 to 3 minutes per side, flipping as necessary, until pale golden brown and cooked through. Using a slotted spoon or a skimmer, transfer to the wire rack or paper towels to drain.

7. Arrange the warm loukoumades on a platter. Drizzle generously with the honey. Sprinkle with the chopped nuts and dust lightly with cinnamon.

SFENJ

MAKES 20 SFENJ

Made from a light, eggy yeast dough flavored with orange juice and zest, these rings can be cut out with a doughnut cutter or stretched free-form by hand. They are typically served by Moroccan Jews as part of the eight-day Hanukkah celebration.

½ cup fresh orange juice

1 package (2¼ teaspoons) active dry yeast

3⅓ cups unbleached all-purpose flour

¼ cup granulated sugar

Grated zest of 1 orange

2 large eggs

4 tablespoons melted butter or vegetable oil

Vegetable oil for deep-frying

Powdered sugar for dusting

1. In a small saucepan, warm half of the orange juice to 110° or 115°F. Remove from the heat and sprinkle with the yeast, 3 tablespoons of the flour, and 1 teaspoon of the granulated sugar. Whisk until smooth, then cover and set aside for 20 minutes, until the mixture is foamy. In a small bowl, rub the orange zest into the remaining granulated sugar.

2. Add the remaining flour to the bowl of a stand mixer fitted with a dough hook. Add the orange sugar, eggs, and melted butter. Beat on medium speed for 1 minute, then add the yeast mixture. Continue beating, adding the remaining ¼ cup of orange juice as needed until the mixture forms as soft dough. (You may not need all of the juice.)

CONTINUED ------------→

3. Reduce the speed to low and knead with dough hook for 4 to 6 minutes, or until dough is smooth and elastic.

4. Transfer to a lightly oiled bowl. Turn the dough to coat it with oil. Cover with a damp clean kitchen towel or plastic wrap and let rise in a warm place for 1½ hours, or until doubled in size.

5. Lightly flour a work surface and a baking sheet. Gently punch the dough down and turn it out on the floured work surface. Using a rolling pin, roll the dough into a ½-inch-thick round. Using a doughnut cutter, cut out rings, flouring the cutter between each cut, and stretching each ring slightly to widen the hole. Arrange the rounds on the floured baking sheet and cover with a dry clean kitchen towel. Let rise in a warm place for 30 minutes, or until puffed and light.

6. In a Dutch oven or other deep, heavy pot, heat 2 to 3 inches oil over medium-high heat to 350°F on a candy or fryer thermometer. Place a grid-patterned wire rack on a baking sheet, or line the pan with two layers of paper towels.

7. Using a slotted spoon or a skimmer, drop the rings into the oil in batches, taking care not to crowd the pan. Fry for 1 or 2 minutes, then flip over to brown the other side for another minute or so, or until golden brown and cooked through.

8. Using a slotted spoon or a skimmer, transfer the rings to the wire rack or paper towels to drain and cool slightly.

9. Transfer the rings to a platter and dust with powdered sugar. Serve warm or at room temperature.

CARDAMOM DOUGHNUTS WITH ROSE SYRUP

MAKES 12 DOUGHNUTS

Rose hips, the plump, reddish-orange fruits of the rose plant, are mouth-puckeringly tart, but also high in vitamin C. They add a zingy tang to the soaking syrup for these spiced Turkish doughnuts, redolent of cardamom and cinnamon. Look for dried rose hips in natural foods stores, or open up a few bags of rose hip tea.

ROSE SYRUP

1 cup water

1 cup sugar

⅓ cup honey

⅓ cup dried rose hips

1 teaspoon whole cardamom pods

¼ cup rose water

2 tablespoons fresh lemon juice

DOUGHNUTS

1 cup unbleached all-purpose flour

½ teaspoon ground cardamom

¼ teaspoon ground cinnamon

1 cup water

½ cup (1 stick) unsalted butter, cut into 8 pieces

1½ tablespoons sugar

½ teaspoon salt

3 large eggs

Vegetable oil for deep-frying

2 tablespoons pistachio nuts (optional), for serving

1. FOR THE SYRUP: In a medium saucepan, bring the water, sugar, honey, rose hips, and cardamom pods to a boil over medium heat, swirling the pan to dissolve the sugar. Reduce the heat to low and simmer for 25 minutes, or until the rose hips are softened and the mixture is fragrant. Remove from the heat, let cool for 5 minutes, then add the rose water and lemon juice. Set aside.

2. FOR THE DOUGHNUTS: Sift the flour and spices together into a medium bowl. In a medium saucepan, combine the water, butter, sugar, and salt. Bring to a boil over medium-high heat, then reduce the heat to low. Using a

CONTINUED

wooden spoon, stir in the flour and cook, stirring constantly, until the mixture pulls away from the sides of the pan and forms a ball.

3. Remove from the heat and let cool for 1 minute. Beat in the eggs, one at a time, beating vigorously and making sure each egg is thoroughly absorbed before adding the next. At first, the mixture will be slippery and resistant, but persist; each egg will be easier to beat in than the one before it.

4. In a Dutch oven or other deep, heavy pot, heat 2 to 3 inches oil over medium-high heat to 350°F on a candy or frying thermometer. Place a grid-patterned wire rack on a baking sheet, or line the pan with two layers of paper towels.

5. Lightly flour a work surface and a baking sheet. While the oil is heating, turn the dough out onto the floured work surface and divide it into 12 pieces. Roll each piece into a ball, then flatten with the heel of your hand. Poke your thumb into the center of each ball and stretch gently to form a ring. Transfer the rings to the floured baking sheet.

6. Using a slotted spoon or a skimmer, drop the rings into the hot oil in batches, being careful not to crowd the pan. Fry for 2 to 3 minutes, then flip and cook on other side for another 2 minutes, or until golden brown and cooked through but still moist inside.

7. Using a slotted spoon or a skimmer, transfer the doughnuts to the wire rack or paper towels to drain. Strain the syrup into a small saucepan, discarding the solids; warm gently over low heat.

8. Arrange the doughnuts on a platter and drizzle with syrup until moistened but not soggy. Serve warm, with remaining syrup on the side for dunking. Sprinkle with pistachio nuts, if desired.

AWWAMAT

MAKES 10 AWWAMAT

This simple yogurt-based dough, similar to that of Indian jalebis, is used in Lebanon to make awwamat, golden balls popular with Lebanese children during the Christmas season. A spiced honey glaze adds sweetness after frying; the balls can also be drizzled with plain warmed honey. LABNE *(also spelled labneh or labna) is also known as yogurt cheese or kefir cheese; it's a thick, spreadable yogurt or kefir that's been drained of its whey. Substitute Greek yogurt if you can't find it.*

GLAZE

1 cup honey

¼ cup water

1 cinnamon stick

2 tablespoons fresh lemon juice

BATTER

1 cup labne or plain Greek yogurt

¼ teaspoon baking soda

Pinch of salt

1½ to 2 cups unbleached all-purpose flour

Vegetable oil for deep-frying

1. FOR THE GLAZE: In a small saucepan, bring the honey, water, cinnamon stick, and lemon juice to a boil over medium heat. Reduce the heat to low and simmer for 2 minutes. Remove from the heat and set aside.

2. FOR THE BATTER: In a medium bowl, beat the labne until smooth. Whisk in the baking soda and salt. Quickly stir in the flour ½ cup at a time to make a smooth, thick batter a little thicker than muffin batter. (You may not need all the flour.)

3. In a Dutch oven or other deep, heavy pot, heat 2 to 3 inches oil over medium-high heat to 325°F on a candy or frying thermometer. Place a grid-patterned wire rack on a baking sheet, or line the pan with two layers of paper towels.

4. Dip 2 tablespoons into the hot oil. Scoop a tablespoonful of batter in one spoon, then use the other spoon to push the batter off the spoon into the hot oil. Repeat, working in batches and being careful not to crowd the pan.

5. Fry for 4 to 5 minutes, flipping as needed to ensure even browning, or until the rounds are golden brown and cooked through but still moist inside. Using a slotted spoon or a skimmer, transfer the rounds to the wire rack or paper towels to drain and cool slightly. Warm the honey syrup over low heat.

6. Arrange the doughnuts on a platter. Drizzle the warm honey syrup over the doughnuts and serve. Any extra syrup can be offered alongside for dipping.

BÁNH CAM

MAKES 24 BÁNH CAM

These delicate Vietnamese doughnuts, filled with sweetened mung bean paste, go well with fragrant jasmine tea for an afternoon snack or dessert. Look for mung beans in Southeast Asian grocery stores; some supermarkets with well-stocked Asian sections may also carry them. Note that the mung beans need to soak overnight before cooking.

½ cup mung beans, soaked in water to cover overnight

3 cups water, plus more as needed

½ cup sugar

3 cups sweet rice flour (mochiko); see note, page 156

½ cup rice flour

1 large boiling potato, boiled, peeled, and mashed (about 1 cup)

⅓ cup sesame seeds

Vegetable oil for deep-frying

1. Drain the mung beans, transfer them to a medium saucepan, and add 2 cups of the water. Add ¼ cup of the sugar and bring to a boil over medium heat, stirring until the sugar is dissolved. Reduce the heat to medium-low and simmer, adding small amounts of water as necessary to keep the beans from scorching, for 15 to 20 minutes, or until the mung beans are soft and all the water has been absorbed. Remove from the heat and let cool briefly.

2. In a blender or food processor, puree the beans to a smooth paste. Scrape into a small bowl and set aside.

CONTINUED ┈┈┈┈┈┈→

3. In a large bowl, stir the remaining ¼ cup sugar together with the rice flours. Add the mashed potato and beat well. Add some of the remaining 1 cup water, a few tablespoons at a time, to make a moist dough. (You may not need all the water.)

4. Lightly flour a work surface and a baking sheet. Turn the dough out onto the floured work surface and divide the dough into 24 pieces. Roll each piece into a ball, then flatten with the heel of your hand into a disk.

5. Place about ½ teaspoon mung bean paste in the center of each disk. Gather the edges up over the filling and gently squeeze into a ball.

6. Pour the sesame seeds into a wide, shallow bowl. Roll each ball in the sesame seeds to coat.

7. In a Dutch oven or other deep, heavy pot, heat 2 to 3 inches oil over medium-high heat to 350°F on a candy or frying thermometer. Place a grid-patterned rack on a baking sheet, or line the pan with two layers of paper towels.

8. Using a slotted spoon or a skimmer, add the balls to the hot oil in batches, being careful not to crowd the pan. Fry, turning as necessary, for 1 to 2 minutes, or until golden brown and cooked through. Using a slotted spoon or a skimmer, transfer the balls to the wire rack or paper towels to drain. Serve warm.

NOTE: Sweet rice flour (also known by its Japanese name, mochiko) is made from short-grain, glutinous rice, the same rice used as "sticky rice" in many Asian dishes. It has a higher starch content than the long-grain rice used in regular rice flour, which makes it particularly good for thickening dough, batters, and sauces. Look for it in Asian grocery stores or in the baking aisle of specialty markets.

GULAB JAMUN

MAKES 10 GULAB JAMUN

One of India's best-known sweets, these balls are soaked in sugar syrup after being fried until they swell to twice their original size. Traditionally, the dough for gulab jamun was made with KHOYA, an Indian version of condensed milk, made from milk slowly cooked until almost solid. Khoya can be found in many Indian grocery stores, but these days, many gulab jamun recipes call for powdered milk, which is easier to find. For best results, use a good-quality full-fat powdered milk.

DOUGH

½ cup powdered whole milk

2 tablespoons unbleached all-purpose flour

¼ teaspoon baking soda

1 tablespoon ghee (Indian-style clarified butter) or unsalted butter, melted

¼ cup whole milk

SYRUP

1¼ cups sugar

1¼ cups water

3 whole green cardamom pods, crushed

6 to 8 threads saffron (optional)

1 teaspoon rose water

Vegetable oil or ghee for deep-frying

1. FOR THE DOUGH: In a medium bowl, combine the powdered milk, flour, and baking soda and stir with a whisk to blend. Using a wooden spoon, stir in the ghee and half of the milk, adding remaining milk a tablespoon at a time as needed to make a soft, smooth dough. Cover bowl and let stand for 20 minutes.

2. Meanwhile, make the syrup: In a medium saucepan, bring the sugar, water, cardamom pods, and saffron, if using, to a boil over medium heat, swirling the pan to dissolve the

PG. 157

CONTINUED ⟶

sugar. Reduce the heat to a simmer and cook for 8 to 10 minutes, swirling occasionally, until thickened slightly to form a light syrup. Remove from the heat and let cool for 5 minutes, then stir in the rose water. Pour the syrup into a deep bowl.

3. To form the dough balls, scoop a tablespoonful of dough into the palm of your hand. Roll between your palms into a small ball. Place the ball on a plate and cover with a damp towel. Repeat with the remaining dough.

4. In a Dutch oven or other deep, heavy pot, heat 2 to 3 inches oil over medium-high heat to 325°F on a candy or frying thermometer. Place a grid-patterned wire rack on a baking sheet, or line the pan with two layers of paper towels.

5. Using a slotted spoon, drop the balls into the hot oil in batches, being careful not to crowd the pan. Reduce the heat to medium. The balls should sink to the bottom of the pot and fry for about 2 minutes, then float up to the surface by themselves. If they don't, you may need to loosen them gently with a slotted spoon. Continue

frying, turning the balls as they fry to ensure even browning, for another 2 to 3 minutes, or until golden brown and cooked through but still moist inside.

6. Using a slotted spoon or a skimmer, transfer each batch of the balls to the wire rack or paper towels to drain briefly, then drop them into the bowl of syrup. Let the balls soak in syrup for at least 1 hour or up to 6 hours before serving.

हिन्दू
खुश – दिल होटल
रेलवे स्टेशन से ५ मिनट का रास्ता
सिगल व डबल कमरे के साथ बाथ रूम
मेन चांदनी चोक
शुद्ध वेजीटेरियन का प्रबन्ध

JALEBIS

MAKES 10 TO 12 JALEBIS

India's version of funnel cakes, these crispy twirls and curls should be served hot from the fryer, after a brief dip in just enough sugar syrup to glaze and moisten them. For best results, use an all-natural, preferably organic, yogurt made without pectin, gelatin, or other thickeners. Note that the batter needs to rest for at least 6 hours or up to 24 hours before frying.

1 cup unbleached all-purpose flour

1 cup plain natural yogurt without thickeners, beaten until smooth

2 to 4 tablespoons water

ROSE SYRUP

1 cup water

1 cup plus 1½ tablespoons sugar

6 to 8 threads saffron (optional)

1 teaspoon rose water (optional)

½ teaspoon salt

Vegetable oil for deep-frying

1. TO START THE BATTER: Add the flour to a medium bowl and make a well in the center. Add the yogurt and mix well with a wooden spoon. Begin stirring in the water, a tablespoon at a time, until you have a smooth, thick batter a little heavier than pancake batter.

2. Cover the bowl and let stand at room temperature for at least 6 hours or up to 24 hours.

3. FOR THE SYRUP: In a small, heavy saucepan, bring the water, 1 cup of the sugar, and saffron, if using, to a simmer over medium heat, swirling the pot to dissolve the sugar. Reduce the heat to medium-low and simmer for 8 to 10 minutes, swirling the pan occasionally, until the mixture has thickened slightly to form a light syrup. Remove from the heat and let cool for 5 minutes, then stir in the rose water, if using. Set aside. Beat the remaining 1½ tablespoons sugar and the salt into the batter.

4. In a Dutch oven or other deep, heavy pot, heat 2 to 3 inches oil over medium-high heat to 325°F on a candy or fryer thermometer. Place a grid-patterned wire rack on a baking sheet, or line the pan with two layers of paper towels. Over low heat, reheat the syrup gently until warm.

5. Spoon the batter into a pastry bag fitted with a ½-inch plain tip. Holding the bag a few inches above the oil, squeeze out a steady stream of batter to make 3 or 4 overlapping loops while moving the bag in a circular motion.

6. Lift the bag up and repeat as necessary to make a small batch of jalebis, being careful not to crowd the pan. Fry for about 60 seconds, or until puffed and beginning to brown. Flip them over and continue cooking for another 60 seconds, continuing to flip and fry as needed, for a total of about 3 minutes, or until the jalebis are a deep golden brown. Using a slotted spoon or a skimmer, transfer the jalebis to the pot of warm syrup. Turn to coat, then transfer to a serving platter. Serve warm.

KOAT PITHAS

MAKES 10 KOAT PITHAS

Jaggery, an unrefined sweetener made from palm or cane syrup, is sold in cakes or chunks in markets specializing in Indian and Southeast Asian products. If jaggery is unavailable, Mexican piloncillo or dark brown sugar can be substituted. Coconut oil is particularly good for frying these Indian doughnuts. If you like the combination of banana and coconut, you can add a small amount of shredded coconut to the batter.

1 cup mashed very ripe bananas (about 2 bananas)

½ cup grated jaggery or piloncillo, or packed dark brown sugar

½ cup rice flour

Generous pinch of salt

2 tablespoons shredded coconut (optional)

A few drops coconut extract (optional)

Coconut oil or vegetable oil for deep-frying

1. In a medium bowl, stir the bananas and jaggery together with a wooden spoon. Sift in the rice flour and salt. Beat the mixture until blended. Stir in the coconut and coconut extract, if using.

2. In a Dutch oven or deep, heavy pot, heat 2 to 3 inches oil over medium-high heat to 325°F on a candy or frying thermometer. Place a grid-patterned wire rack on a baking sheet, or line the pan with two layers of paper towels.

3. Dip 2 tablespoons into the hot oil. Working in batches and taking care not to crowd the pan, scoop up 1 tablespoonful of batter in one spoon, then use the other spoon to push the batter off the spoon into the hot oil.

4. Fry, flipping as needed to ensure even browning, for 3 to 4 minutes, or until the pithas are golden brown and cooked through but still moist inside.

5. Using a slotted spoon or a skimmer, transfer the pithas to the wire rack or paper towels to drain. Serve warm.

BONELOS AGAS

MAKES 12 TO 14 BONELOS

If you grew up in a place where bananas didn't grow on trees, you might be excused for thinking that there's only one type of banana: the big, crescent-shaped yellow Cavendish variety found in every U.S. supermarket from coast to coast. But as anyone from the Pacific islands can tell you, there are dozens and dozens of different bananas out there, from fluffy, finger-sized ice cream bananas and apple bananas to red-skinned bananas and many more, each with its own unique flavor. Bonelos are similar to Mexican-style buñuelos (page 97), only these small, round fritters from the island of Guam are made from a base of sweetened banana.

1½ **cups mashed very ripe bananas (about 3 bananas)**

⅓ **cup sugar**

1 **teaspoon vanilla extract**

1⅓ **cups unbleached all-purpose flour**

1 **teaspoon baking powder**

Pinch of salt

Vegetable oil for deep-frying

1. In a medium bowl and using a wooden spoon, beat the bananas, sugar, and vanilla together.

2. Sift the flour, baking powder, and salt together into a small bowl. Stir into the banana mixture to make a soft, thick batter about the texture of muffin batter.

3. In a Dutch oven or other deep, heavy pot, heat 2 to 3 inches oil over medium-high heat to 350°F on a candy or fryer thermometer. Place a grid-patterned wire rack on a baking sheet, or line the pan with two layers of paper towels.

4. Dip 2 tablespoons into the hot oil. Working in batches and taking care not to crowd the pan, scoop up a tablespoonful of batter in one spoon, then use the other spoon to push the batter off the spoon into the hot oil.

5. Fry, flipping as needed to ensure even browning, for 3 to 4 minutes, or until the bonelos are golden brown and cooked through but still moist inside.

6. Using a slotted spoon or a skimmer, transfer the bonelos to the wire rack or paper towels to drain. Serve warm.

INDEX

TABLE OF EQUIVALENTS

THE EXACT EQUIVALENTS IN THE FOLLOWING TABLES
HAVE BEEN ROUNDED FOR CONVENIENCE.

LIQUID/DRY MEASUREMENTS

U.S.	METRIC
¼ teaspoon	1.25 milliliters
½ teaspoon	2.5 milliliters
1 teaspoon	5 milliliters
1 tablespoon (3 teaspoons)	15 milliliters
1 fluid ounce (2 tablespoons)	30 milliliters
¼ cup	60 milliliters
⅓ cup	80 milliliters
½ cup	120 milliliters
1 cup	240 milliliters
1 pint (2 cups)	480 milliliters
1 quart (4 cups, 32 ounces)	960 milliliters
1 gallon (4 quarts)	3.84 liters
1 ounce (by weight)	28 grams
1 pound	454 grams
2.2 pounds	1 kilogram

LENGTHS

U.S.	METRIC
⅛ inch	3 millimeters
¼ inch	6 millimeters
½ inch	12 millimeters
1 inch	2.5 centimeters

OVEN TEMPERATURE

FAHRENHEIT	CELSIUS	GAS
250	120	½
275	140	1
300	150	2
325	160	3
350	180	4
375	190	5
400	200	6
425	220	7
450	230	8
475	240	9
500	260	10